MONMOUTHSHIRE

CURIOSITIES

MONMOUTHSHIRE
CURIOSITIES

MIKE HALL

The
History
Press

First published 2010

The History Press
The Mill, Brimscombe Port
Stroud, Gloucestershire, GL5 2QG
www.thehistorypress.co.uk

© Mike Hall, 2010

The right of Mike Hall to be identified as the Author
of this work has been asserted in accordance with the
Copyrights, Designs and Patents Act 1988.

British Library Cataloguing in Publication Data.
A catalogue record for this book is available from the British Library.

ISBN 978 0 7524 4899 2

Typesetting and origination by The History Press
Printed in India, Aegean Offset
Manufacturing managed by Jellyfish Print Solutions Ltd

Contents

A King's Head at the King's Head

The King's Head Hotel presents a largely eighteenth-century front to Agincourt Square in the centre of Monmouth but behind it is at least a century older. To the left of the entrance there is a small bar with a fine seventeenth-century plaster ceiling, featuring a large rose surmounted by a wreath with four smaller ones in the corners. On the overmantel above the fireplace is a painted plaster figure of Charles II, which is a rare survival. He is portrayed crowned and robed. Alongside in the plasterwork are his initials and two pots of roses. The rest of the bar's décor hardly lives up to this but it is well worth visiting nevertheless.

In April 1972 I stayed at the King's Head as one of a group of trainee geography teachers from London University. After our long journey west we queued patiently to collect our room keys. My colleague Nigel Bailey and I were at the back of the line and were offered two keys by the receptionist. Nigel was somewhat annoyed to find himself billeted in what he described as 'little more than a broom cupboard'. It took longer to locate my room. When I finally found it I opened the door to be confronted by an elegant four-poster bed, topped by a curved and frilly white lace canopy. The room was light and sensual. It was clear that I had, by chance, been allocated the Bridal Suite, which I was to occupy in solitary splendour!

The news quickly spread and in a group of healthy young men and women, albeit training to be mature and sensible role models, there were inevitably ribald comments and suggestions, but I felt that my fiancée Linda, blissfully unaware in Bristol, would hardly approve if I acted upon them. The following year I tried to book this room for our honeymoon but sadly it was already taken.

Such was my introduction to the curiosities of Monmouthshire!

Charles II plasterwork at the King's Head, Monmouth.

For this book I have divided historic Monmouthshire into areas easily explored from its main centres. Although some well-known places are included, I have omitted others that have been extensively described elsewhere, in order to direct readers to sites that they might not have heard of otherwise.

The selection is personal. I did not manage to get absolutely everywhere. One place I regret not visiting is the little church of Holy Cross, Kilgwrrwg, which has, among other curiosities, the grave of Richard Morgan, the last sailor to be killed in the First World War. John Kinross in *Discovering the Smallest Churches in Wales* writes that 'to reach this little church is a real pilgrimage ... the hill drops alarmingly to a rambling farm where you should park and ask for directions. You need boots.'

This book could not have been written without the unwitting assistance of previous writers on the county. Often they capture the spirit of the place better than I could do. I have taken the liberty of quoting them directly where this is the case. In particular I should mention the Monmouthshire volume in Arthur Mee's *The King's England* series (published in 1951, since when its title has become outdated in two respects!). Much of it was in fact completed by Hugo Tyerman and Sydney Warner after Mee's death but it was simpler to ascribe all quotations to Mee himself. The Gwent section of Simon Jenkins' recent book on Wales was also essential topographical reading.

The articles by Fred Hando, which originally appeared in the *South Wales Argus*, published in a series of books during the 1950s (and more recent collections), describe a world we have sadly lost. John Newman's 'Gwent/Monmouthshire' in *The Buildings of Wales* series (an update of the classic Pevsner architectural guides) directed me to places of interest I might have missed and provided a backbone of factual rigour that I undoubtedly needed. For Newport, Ann Drysdale's *Real Newport* was invaluable. Articles in the *Argus* alerted me to recent developments.

Any errors are, of course, all mine! Unless otherwise stated, all photographs are by Mike or Linda Hall.

INTRODUCTION

Monmouthshire: England or Wales?

The status of Monmouthshire is a curiosity in itself. When I did geography O-level in 1966, it was officially part of England but any Act of Parliament intended to apply to Wales only, specifically included Monmouthshire as well. Government statistics always referred to 'Wales and Monmouthshire'. Towns with unambiguously Welsh place names, such as Pontypool, Abersychan, Blaenavon and Nantyglo, were nevertheless still officially in England.

Monmouthshire Council
Offices, Cwmbran.

This odd state of affairs dated from the second Act of Union of 1543 when the county of Monmouthshire, made up from several former Marcher Lordships (created centuries before by the Normans to control and subdue the Welsh), was included in the Oxford judicial circuit for legal purposes, while the other twelve Welsh counties were placed in four Welsh circuits!

In 1972 a bill to reform local government in England and Wales came before Parliament. The issue of Monmouthshire was totally absent from the minds of the legislators who drafted it. Their main aim was to create new and supposedly more relevant and efficient authorities, such as Avon, Humberside and Greater Manchester. These proved to be extremely unpopular, some were short-lived and most people retain their loyalties to the historic counties to this day. In the course of a debate on the bill, Mr Brynmor John, the MP for Pontypridd, moved an amendment which stated that Monmouthshire and the County Borough of Newport should henceforward be part of Wales for all purposes. At an all-night sitting on 20 July the government minister responsible, Mr Gibson-Watt, confirmed that the argument was over and that Monmouthshire was 'part of Wales for good and for ever'.

This was too much for an eminent English MP. 'Hansard' reports that Mr Gerald Kaufman (Manchester Ardwick) asked, 'Am I to take it that an annexation of this magnitude is to be carried through a sparsely attended House of Commons on the nod at five minutes to midnight? I wish to voice my protest.' His protest was in vain.

And so it came to pass that on 1 April 1974 Monmouthshire, renamed Gwent, became part of Wales and, after Devolution in the 1990s, residents of totally Anglicized places such as Newport, Sudbrook, Shirenewton and Redwick found themselves with representatives sitting in a Welsh Assembly in Cardiff and, potentially at least, the opportunity to vote for Plaid Cymru!

The story does not end there. In 1996 the five districts of Gwent became unitary authorities, responsible for the provision of all local services. These were the County Borough of Newport; Torfaen, Caerphilly and Blaenau Gwent (three councils covering small, densely-populated areas in the valleys of the coalfield); and Monmouth, the rural two-thirds in the eastern part of the old county. Caerphilly Council (formerly Islwyn) now included areas in part of Monmouthshire, although Caerphilly itself had been in Glamorgan. To add to the confusion the Monmouth Council area was re-christened Monmouthshire and the name Gwent was abolished! However, it survives in many places, not least the masthead of the *South Wales Argus* whose headline-writers find it a useful shorthand to describe its circulation area.

Strictly speaking therefore the use of 'Monmouthshire' in the title of this book – which covers all of the historic county – is incorrect. Anything more accurate would have been something of a mouthful. I have also been somewhat inconsistent in that I have included Brynmawr (formerly in Breconshire) but not Caerphilly.

Archdeacon Coxe – an Illustrious Predecessor

In addition to the authors already mentioned, any writer describing places of interest in the county owes a debt to the intrepid Archdeacon Coxe, whose *Historical Tour of Monmouthshire* was published in 1801.

Archdeacon William Coxe MA was one of those leisured eighteenth-century clergymen whose duties were apparently light enough to allow for him to devote a great deal of time to learned and antiquarian pursuits. Born in Dover Street, Piccadilly, in 1747, the son of the Physician to the King's Household, he was educated at Marylebone Grammar School (from the age of five), Eton and King's College, Cambridge. Ordained in 1771, he then secured a series of posts as tutor to the sons of the nobility, affording him the opportunity to travel extensively in Europe. He published a number of books describing these excursions in great detail. In 1788 he became Rector of Bemerton in Wiltshire and Prebendary of Salisbury Cathedral in 1791. In 1803 he married Eleanora, daughter of Britain's Consul-General in St Petersburg and the following year became Archdeacon of Wiltshire. He died in 1828 and is buried in the church at Bemerton.

The *Historical Tour of Monmouthshire* was based on excursions undertaken in 1798 and 1799 with his friend Sir Richard Hoare Bt. 'I was delighted with the picturesque ruins of ancient castles memorable in the annals of history,' he wrote, 'and I was animated by the views of mansions distinguished by the residence of illustrious persons.'

Like all authors, he had his problems completing his task. 'Want of time and unfavourable weather prevented me from visiting the sequestered and mountainous districts,' he wrote and felt obliged to undertake a third expedition in the autumn of 1799: 'In the three journeys I employed five months and traversed 1,500 miles and now present to the public the result of my observations and researches.'

Archdeacon Coxe.

Much of the book is taken up with genealogical details of the aristocratic families whose great houses he visited and also with political and constitutional history but the greater interest lies in the topographical descriptions of Monmouthshire at a time when the effects of the Industrial Revolution were just starting to transform parts of the county for ever.

The noble archdeacon was not averse to indulging in pedantic scholarly bickering. In a footnote concerning the ancient earthworks by the Severn at Sudbrook he writes of an earlier author that 'Harris, in his account of this entrenchment is extremely erroneous. He describes it as square, with the church standing in the middle. The word "square" has induced many authors, who have never seen it, to consider it Roman. Harris deserves applause for having first turned the public attention to the antiquities of Monmouthshire but I am concerned to add that I have found many of his descriptions extremely inaccurate … I think it necessary to make this observation because his accounts have been servilely copied by superficial writers.' I can almost feel him looking over my shoulder and tut-tutting with exasperation as I do the same!

But I warm to him when he writes of the Roman period that he was 'too conscious of my scanty acquaintance with this branch of antiquities, and the difficulty of the subject, not to be apprehensive that the antiquary will find great deficiency in this part of the work'.

I sympathised with his attack of vertigo on the ridge of the Skirrid Mountain (*see* p.47) and with his disclaimer that 'the reader must not expect to find a regular history of Monmouthshire but [merely] a description of the principal places, intermixed with historical relations and biographical anecdotes.'

That is more or less what he or she will find in this book!

Mike Hall, October 2009

1

Chepstow, the Wye Valley & Monmouth

WASSAILING AND THE MARI LWYD
CHEPSTOW

The passing of the old year and the coming of the new have always been a time for celebration and rituals – often fuelled by large amounts of alcohol. In England it was often wassailing and in Wales there was the tradition of the Mari Lwyd, a mysterious figure that went from house to house, accompanied by singers and musicians.

The Mari Lwyd was like the morris dancers' hobby horse, incorporating a real horse's skull. With various costumed attendants, it toured the villages at night. As they approached a house the doors would be barred, traditional songs and greetings were exchanged before the door was opened and the Mari Lwyd and party were admitted for refreshments and the exchange of gifts.

Not everyone approved. In his book *The Folklore of (old) Monmouthshire* (Logaston Press, 1998) folklorist Roy Palmer quotes William Roberts, a Baptist minister, who wrote in 1852 that people should 'withdraw their support from such old Pagan and Popish ceremonies which have come down from the darkest ages in learning, behaviour and religion. I wish of this folly, and similar follies, that they find no place anywhere apart from the museum.'

Appropriately, the English and Welsh traditions have recently been combined in the annual Two Rivers Folk Wassail and Mari Lwyd held in the border town of Chepstow on a Saturday in early January. The festivities include morris dancing throughout the town and children's events near the castle and the bandstand. In the early evening Mari Lwyd processions from both the English and Welsh sides meet in the middle of the old bridge over the River Wye. On a fine night it is a magical event.

The Mari Lwyd.

Another local New Year custom, the Calennig, was described by the writer Arthur Machen:

> When I was a boy [he was born in 1863], there was a very queer celebration in Caerleon, the little Monmouthshire town where I was born. The children got the biggest and bravest and gayest apple they could find in the loft. They put bits of gold leaf upon it, they stuck raisins into it. They inserted into the apple little sprigs of box and then they deliberately slit the ends of hazel nuts so that the nuts appeared to grow from the ends of the box leaves. Three bits of stick were fixed into the base of the apple, tripod-wise and so it was borne round from house to house. The children got cakes and sweets and cups of ale.

It sounds rather like the Wassail bowl that can still be seen at Chepstow to this day, and also like the recently-revived Christingle.

According to Roy Palmer, at Chepstow the Calennig was called a 'monty' (from 'good morn to ye', an orange was used instead of an apple and holly instead of box. 'Between six a.m. and noon boys and girls went from house to house chanting: "Monty, Monty, happy New Year. A pocket full of money and a cellar full of beer".'

The custom had died out by 1914 (and I cannot see modern children reviving a custom which has such an early start!) but Fred Hando wrote of being given a Calennig early in the Second World War by a lady brought up in Chepstow who told him not to remove the orange 'until it was quite withered, whereupon I should see a happy year'. A similar custom apparently still survives at Devauden.

Chepstow also hosts a weekend festival in mid-July with more music and dancing, as well as concerts with many of the top performers in the world of folk music. Full details can be obtained from www.tworiversfolkfestival.com.

LEST WE FORGET
CHEPSTOW WAR MEMORIAL

With its Army base virtually under the older Severn Bridge at Beachley, Chepstow is very much a garrison town and, like Wootton Bassett in Wiltshire, knows how to commemorate those brave men and women who serve their country. On 21 May 2009 the streets were thronged for the Homecoming Parade of the 1st Rifles, returning from Afghanistan.

Chepstow is one of the few places in Britain whose War Memorial sees ceremonies to mark Anzac Day and the Gallipoli campaign, in addition to Remembrance Day. For about ten years now local people have gathered to remember Able Seaman William Charles Williams who was posthumously awarded the Victoria Cross for his heroism at Gallipoli. At this ceremony, attended by the mayor, members

U-boat gun, Chepstow.

of the Royal British Legion, Royal Naval Association and the Royal Engineers, members of Able Seaman Williams' family lay wreaths in his memory.

During the Allied landings there in April 1915, Able Seaman Williams held on to a rope securing a floating pontoon for over an hour, under fire the whole time. His action prevented the pontoon from drifting away and enabled the soldiers to disembark from their ship. The official VC citation reads 'He was eventually dangerously wounded and later killed while his rescue was being effected by his commander, who described him as the bravest soldier he had ever met.'

The gun located next to the War Memorial in Beaufort Square was given to Chepstow by King George V in recognition of Williams' bravery. It came from a captured German submarine. In Chepstow, at least, 'We Will Remember Them'.

A NEW HOME FOR SEVERN VETERAN?

THE SEVERN PRINCESS, *CHEPSTOW*

Long ago, before the Severn Bridge was opened in 1966 there were only two ways to get a car across from Bristol to Chepstow – one was secured (hopefully!) onto a flat wagon on a special train that ran through the tunnel and the other was the Aust to Beachley ferry. Many people have fond memories of this delightfully idiosyncratic service, though there is a famous photograph of the singer Bob Dylan looking very grumpy on the slipway. Perhaps he was in for a long wait due to the state of the tide, or had had a rough crossing.

The last of the boats to operate the service was the *Severn Princess*, built by the Yorkshire Dry Dock Company at Hull, launched on 23 May 1959 and registered at Newport on 9 November 1960. 77ft in length and 28ft wide, she was licensed to carry up to ninety-four passengers and their vehicles but was in service for less than six years.

The *Severn Princess*, due for renovation.

When the Severn Bridge was opened and the ferry service came to an end, she was laid up in Chepstow and later in Cardiff. After being overhauled in Bristol she was sold to the West of Ireland Fisheries Ltd in June 1969. For the next thirty years or so, the *Severn Princess* saw service in Irish waters, being based variously at Foynes, Limerick and Galway.

Somehow she then found her way home. In the spring of 2009 I found her, rusty and forlorn, on a piece of waste ground below the road and rail bridge over the Wye at Chepstow. The vandals had got to her and left their mark. It seemed a sad end.

However on 22 July a Planning Notice appeared in the Classified ads section of the *South Wales Argus*:

> Proposed open space area on derelict land, beneath Brunel-designed bridge, to include performance space, information boards, the renovated *Severn Princess* boat and other sculptural items.

I am not sure how much will have been done before this book is published in 2010 but I hope this scheme succeeds.

MONNOW BRIDGE
MONMOUTH

Monmouth is the main centre for touring the Wye Valley, but when you are in the town centre you are almost totally unaware of the river. This is because the Wye is now cut off from historic Monmouth by the busy A40. Before 1965, when the dual-carriageway was cut through between Monmouth School and the Wye bridge, things must have been very different.

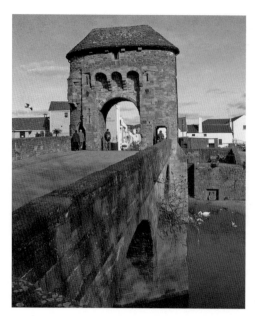

The Monnow Bridge.

It is the Wye's west-bank tributary, the Monnow, which contributes to Monmouth's townscape, or more particularly the medieval bridge that crosses it. It is the only survival in Britain of a gate-tower on a bridge leading into a town, something that was once common throughout Europe.

To feel what it must have been like in the Middle Ages it is best to approach Monmouth on foot through the district still known as Overmonnow, where there is a small but over-restored twelfth-century church of St Thomas. The Old Red Sandstone gateway arched over the roadway looms up in front of you. It dates from a strengthening of Monmouth's town walls and defences around 1300. The pedestrian arches at either side of the main opening are nineteenth century. The room over the gatehouse has had various uses over the centuries: guard-room, powder-chamber and observation post in times of unrest, such as the Civil War in the seventeenth century and the Chartist Riots in the nineteenth.

The bridge itself is believed to date from 1272 and has three arches on hexagonal piers. Tolls were levied on ships unloading here – 3d on every vessel laden with goods for sale and 4d on every bag of wool.

Sadly, some of the buildings close to the bridge are somewhat shabby and, with a car park away to the right, the crowded character of medieval Monmouth is now lost. However, crossing the bridge leads the visitor into Monnow Street with its gracious buildings, mostly dating from the eighteenth or early nineteenth centuries. With the spire of the parish church of St Mary's as a landmark, Monnow Street goes up to Agincourt Square at the heart of the town.

The square is dominated by the impressive Shire Hall. The façade includes a statue of an armour-clad Henry V who was born in Monmouth Castle in 1387.

There is not much of the castle left now, just the ruins of a tower and the Great Hall, but it remained a significant military stronghold until the seventeenth century.

A more recent figure, renowned from a world Henry could never have imagined, is commemorated by a prominent statue in front of Shire Hall. Charles Rolls is best remembered as a pioneer of motoring but here he is seen examining a model of an early biplane, a tribute to his passion for flying – which was to bring about his early death.

Rolls was killed when his plane crashed at a flying demonstration at Bournemouth in 1910 and the memorial was unveiled a year later. Ironically, the tail of the model plane was damaged some years ago when, in a misguided attempt at cleaning it, the statue was sandblasted by council workmen!

GRACIOUS HOUSES OF AN ELEGANT AGE
MONNOW STREET, MONMOUTH

The elegant buildings that grace Monmouth suggest that the town's Golden Age came half a century either side of 1800. Monnow Street has two interesting examples.

One of the finest houses is Cornwall House. Dating from the seventeenth century, it was acquired in 1752 by Henry Burgh, agent to the Duke of Beaufort. He added the fine garden front, facing the open space known, confusingly, as Chippenham. Races took place on this ground and Burgh built a grandstand in the garden of Cornwall House for the duke and his guests. The side of the house facing Monnow Street was refaced in the 1770s.

In the garden behind Lloyd's Bank is a summer-house which has a painted inscription recalling Nelson's visit on 19 August 1802. It is said that the admiral took coffee here before going up the Kymin to inspect the Naval Temple.

The temple, poised high above Monmouth, is (in Newman's words) 'an extraordinary jingoistic structure commemorating the admirals whose naval victories since 1793 had just culminated in Nelson's rout of Napoleon at the Battle of the Nile'. It celebrated 'The Standard of Great Britain waving triumphant over the fallen and captive of France, Spain and Holland'. Even at the time some eminent visitors considered it to be 'in very bad taste'.

Agincourt Square has the King's Head (*see* p.6), the Punch House and the Beaufort Arms, fine inns all of them once, but the latter was converted into shops and flats about twenty years ago. The square (which is actually more triangular in shape) stands in front of the Shire Hall of 1784.

Grander than all is Great Castle House built in 1673 in the castle precinct for Henry Somerset (later the first Duke of Beaufort), described by Newman as 'a house of splendid swagger outside and in.'

But it is the smaller details, as illustrated in the photographs (all taken in or near Monnow Street), that I find most interesting. As in most towns, it is best to look above the modern shop fronts to find the quirky and the curious features that give a place its character.

Houses in Monmouth. The house in the centre photograph has the national emblems of Wales, Ireland, England and Scotland above the upper windows.

A CRYPTIC GRAVESTONE
ST MARY'S CHURCHYARD, MONMOUTH

Roy Palmer's book *The Folklore of (old) Monmouthshire* is a fascinating treasure trove of customs and traditions. Among many other things, it directed me to the strange epitaph of John Rennie in the churchyard of St Mary's, Monmouth.

It comprises 285 letters arranged in a grid reading, in various directions, 'Here lies John Renie'. Missing out the second 'n' in his surname may be deliberate – or perhaps is an error by the stone carver.

```
E I N E R N H O J S J O H N R E N I E
I N E R N H O J S E S J O H N R E N I
N E R N H O J S E I E S J O H N R E N
E R N H O J S E I L I E S J O H N R E
R N H O J S E I L E L I E S J O H N R
N H O J S E I L E R E L I E S J O H N
H O J S E I L E R E R E L I E S J O H
O J S E I L E R E H E R E L I E S J O
H O J S E I L E R E R E L I E S J O H
N H O J S E I L E R E L I E S J O H N
R N H O J S E I L E L I E S J O H N R
E R N H O J S E I L I E S J O H N R E
N E R N H O J S E I E S J O H N R E N
I N E R N H O J S E S J O H N R E N I
E I N E R N H O J S J O H N R E N I E
```

WHO DIED MAY 31 1832
AGED 33 YEARS

It is certainly a nightmare to transcribe. The trick is to follow the letters in each compass direction, starting from the centre. In the end it was all to no avail. At a later date the stone was moved from its original position to a place by the east end of the church – so poor John does not lie 'here' any more!

DOLPHINS AND LITTLE BOYS PLAYING IN THE FOUNTAIN

ST ARVANS

The delightful Victorian drinking fountain at St Arvans, just north of Chepstow Racecourse, will be familiar to anyone travelling on the Wye Valley road. It was set up by Monmouthshire County Council in 1893. Made of cast iron, now painted dark green, it was manufactured by the Sun Foundry in Glasgow and assembled by the Iron Stores Company, Chepstow. Dolphins twist around the structure's central stem and there are the figures of two little boys carrying pots from which the water still issues at the press of a button. There are hooks from which little cups presumably once hung but they do not do so now.

The drinking fountain at St Arvans.

The church is tucked away down a lane in the centre of the village. Largely a nineteenth-century rebuild, it nevertheless is home to some older artefacts, including a cross shaft that may be 1,000 years old. There are fixtures and fittings reflecting the parish's position at the Catholic end of the Anglican spectrum but the item that most caught my attention was the printed notice pinned up directly beneath the obligatory 'No Smoking' notice in the porch. In tones reflecting someone's exasperation at Political Correctness and the Nanny State, it is a memorable rant against the legal requirement to display such an unnecessary injunction!

THE CIRCLE OF LEGENDS
TINTERN

A mile or so upstream from the Abbey six life-sized wooden figures stand close to the River Wye at Tintern Old Station. Known as 'The Circle of Legends', they depict characters from Monmouthshire's history and were created by sculptors Neil Gow and John Hobbs in 2002-3. The statues were commissioned by Monmouthshire County Council's Countryside Service.

Visitors might be surprised to find King Arthur here, associating him with Cornwall or Somerset; but Monmouthshire claims him too. Some historians identify him as Arthurius ap Meurig ap Tewdrig, a legendary King of the Silures.

With the second figure, Eleanor of Provence (1227-1291), we are on firmer ground historically. The younger sister of the Queen of France, she married Henry III and bore him no less than nine children. In Monmouthshire, her influence can be particularly seen at Grosmont (*see* p.33). Queen Eleanor's Chapel in Grosmont Church shows the hand of the architects she brought over from France, as do parts of the castle, notably the chimney that also bears her name.

From an earlier period of history we have Offa, King of Mercia from AD 757 to 796. After his kingdom suffered grievously from Welsh incursions in the 780s, he had a massive earthwork built to define the boundary 'from sea to sea' and defend his territory. Offa's Dyke stretches from the North Wales coast at Prestatyn to the Severn at Sedbury near Chepstow. In this part of the Wye Valley the Dyke followed the line of the cliffs on the opposite bank of the river.

There are two more legendary figures in the circle. Tewdrig, a sixth-century Welsh chieftain murdered by the invading Saxons, and the bare-breasted figure of Sabrina, goddess of the River Severn, known to the Welsh as Hafren. Her legend tells how a married King of England fell in love with Elfridis. The result of their union was a beautiful daughter, Hafren. The jealous queen ordered mother and daughter to be thrown to their deaths in the Severn. Hafren was transformed into a goddess of healing, giving her name to the river.

These stories come from the work of Geoffrey of Monmouth (born 1100). He became Bishop of St Asaph in 1156. His *History of the Kings of Britain*, although

Geoffrey of Monmouth.

not standing up well to modern notions of academic scholarship, is important to historians as it gives a Welsh perspective lacking in other writers of the time. Geoffrey's figure completes the Circle.

There is more information available in one of the carriages alongside the old station, also details of trails showing visitors places in Monmouthshire associated with the six characters commemorated by the sculptures.

'TOWN OF THE STONES'

TRELLECH

Trellech's name derives from its prehistoric monument known as 'Harold's Stones', south-west of the village. These three stones are in line along the side of the ridge, a rare example of a Bronze Age alignment. The footpath leading to the stones has been cut through the meadows alongside the B4293.

Inevitably, various legends have grown up to account for these enigmatic stones. Their name derives from the belief that they commemorate King Harold's victory over the Welsh in 1063, but they are clearly much older than that. Roy Palmer quotes the tale of a stone-throwing contest between the mystical John of Kent (*see* Grosmont, p.33) and the Devil from the top of Trellech Beacon. John threw first, we are told, reaching the outskirts of the village, but was bested by the Devil's first shot. John then made an even longer throw whereupon the Devil, clearly a bad loser, stormed off in disgust.

Above left: Harold's Stones, Trellech.

Above right: The Virtuous Well, Trellech.

Another relic which has attracted various folktales to it is the so-called 'Virtuous Well' in a field alongside the lane towards Tintern. The water bubbles up in an arched recess surrounded by a horseshoe-shaped wall. In the seventeenth century it was described as 'much-frequented and reputed to cure the scurvy, collick and other distempers'. In 1839 a medical man, W.H.Thomas, was recommending the waters to sufferers of 'dyspepsia, hypochondriasis and amenorrhagia', the latter being the absence of menstruation. As quoted in Roy Palmer's book, he went on: 'Little does the proprietor of this neglected fountain, over which the wisdom of our ancestors built a devotional shrine, know the treasure which the Almighty has deposited in our hands or he would gratefully rebuild its ruined walls, cleanse out its channels and invite guests to a festival of health'. In 1951 the walls were indeed rebuilt to mark the Festival of Britain.

It is still a place which exerts old pagan magic. Fairies are said to dance at the well on Midsummer Eve and the story is still told that a farmer who blocked access to it found that, as the wise folk predicted, his land became waterless. It was said that if no bubbles rose from the water when pebbles were thrown in, the wish would not be granted. Aphrodisiac properties have been claimed for the waters. Even now, there are flowers and little dolls in the niches of the stonework. The overhanging branches are festooned with pieces of cloth and when I visited there was even an old sock, evidence of the belief that disease will be discarded along with an item of the sufferer's clothing.

Trellech is now a small village but was once of considerably greater importance as ongoing archaeological research is demonstrating. A planned town created by the de Clare family, in the thirteenth century it was the largest borough in the county, eclipsing Chepstow. The magnificent church is a reminder of its former glories. A severe fire in 1296 heralded Trellech's decline and its upland situation, remote from the rivers that carried much trade at the time, did not help. By 1696 it was merely 'a poore inconsiderable village'. The 1901 census recorded just seventeen inhabited houses. There are not many more even now.

2

Abergavenny
& Usk

A CHURCH THAT IS A CHURCH NO LONGER

ST JOHN'S, ABERGAVENNY

With its sturdy old tower it certainly looks like a church, but it has not been one for nearly 500 years. With the decline of organised religion in the twentieth century, redundant churches are sadly commonplace today, but the history of St John's, Abergavenny, is more unusual and interesting.

The church was deconsecrated in 1542, the time of the Dissolution of the Monasteries by Henry VIII, after the townspeople of Abergavenny bought the chapel of St Mary's Priory to use as their parish church. It was far grander than poor little St John's and they were very pleased with their bargain.

St John's became the King Henry VIII Grammar School. The tower survived intact but the body of the church was absorbed into later buildings. According to Archdeacon Coxe, writing in 1801, the tower was taken down and then rebuilt 'about fifty years ago'. John Newman, who quotes this in *The Buildings of Wales*, describes it as 'a curious piece of antiquarianism for the mid-eighteenth century'.

St John's Church, Abergavenny.

The building continued to be used by the school until 1898 when a new school building was put up on the edge of the town at Penypound. The old building at St John's then became a Masonic Temple. At about the same time, the altar stone from St John's was discovered being used as a lintel in a nearby building. It has been reconsecrated and is now in Holy Trinity Church in Baker Street, a Gothic-style church dating from 1840-2, designed by T.H. Wyatt and put up at the expense of Miss Rachel Herbert.

HOUSE THAT WAS A PRIESTS' REFUGE

GUNTER HOUSE, ABERGAVENNY

During the religiously-turbulent seventeenth century, Gunter House in Cross Street, Abergavenny, was the home of the Gunter family, who were Roman Catholic. Here Thomas Gunter JP sheltered two priests, David Lewis and Philip Evans. It was illegal to practise Catholicism in public and so he had a chapel constructed secretly in the roof space. In 1678, at the time of the anti-Catholic hysteria whipped up after the alleged Titus Oates plot against the life of Charles II, a House of Commons committee was appointed to consider what was then described as 'the danger the Nation is in by the Growth of Popery and for providing Remedies to prevent the same'.

Witnesses from Monmouthshire, including John Arnold Esq., of Llanfihangel Crucorney, William James of Caerleon and Revd Greenhaugh, the vicar of Abergavenny, testified that two Catholic priests, David Lewis and Philip Evans, were being sheltered in Gunter House, the Mass was being said there and weddings and Christenings taking place.

Thomas Gunter was unrepentant. 'I kept a Priest in Oliver Cromwell's time of severity and will keep one now,' he said. Both priests were taken by the authorities and executed. There is a plaque on the front wall of the house commemorating these sad events.

A painting of the Adoration of the Magi, taken down from the plastered wall of the chapel, is now preserved in Abergavenny Museum. In *Out and About in Monmouthshire* Fred Hando told the curious tale of the mural's discovery, disappearance and subsequent rediscovery. It seems that when workmen removed a partition in the top storey of the house in 1907 they discovered the secret chamber which measured 23ft by 10ft. On the sloping ceiling at the east end of the room was the mural which had remained hidden for nearly 250 years. With its underlying plaster, it was carefully removed, placed under glass in an oak frame and taken, as Mr Hando quotes 'into private custody ... and was once again lost to view. Inquiries made in recent years,' he wrote in 1958, 'were fruitless'.

But then, as he records, a shopkeeper discovered the framed mural hidden behind a dresser and it has subsequently found its way into the care of the museum.

Gunter's House, Abergavenny.

He describes it thus:

> Under the black roof on the right is the ox, rendered with the poise and
> forthright technique of a prehistoric cave-painting. Dressed in deep blue,
> the Virgin Mary, with a circlet halo above her head, nurses the Holy Child,
> whose halo is more ornate. The star in the east directs its rays towards the
> Child. On the left is a Wise man with a hypnotic eye.

Fred Hando describes visiting Mrs Francis, an eighty-one-year-old lady who
remembered the alterations being made to Gunter House in 1907. In addition to the
fresco, the initials 'T.G.' were found on the partition and high on the wall above the
attic window were painted the letters 'IHS' – the mark of the Jesuits – and a heart
coloured red on a green oval surrounded by golden rays and surmounted by a cross.

'A WORK OF ART, VISIBLE FOR MILES'
ABERGAVENNY TOWN HALL

Abergavenny is dominated not by its castle, or the magnificent Priory Church,
but by the Town Hall, a grandiloquent structure redolent of Victorian municipal
pride. Its tall campanile-style tower capped by a green copper pyramid can be
seen for miles around. It actually looks better from a distance; close to it is bulky
and bullying, but an impressive edifice for all that.

It was designed by Bath-based architects Wilson & Willcox, who won a competition in 1869 to design a replacement for the existing building. Not only does it house the usual municipal offices but also the town's indoor market and a theatre. Playgoers reach the auditorium by means of a handsome staircase passing a door labelled 'Mayor's Parlour' as well as imposing lists of civic dignitaries and sobering lists of local men and women who died in the service of their country. The theatre, renovated in about 1990, is an intimate venue with handsome décor and good acoustics.

The council chamber itself is lit by the glazed heads of the arcade on the main front. The indoor market is housed in a light utilitarian hall with a pitched roof supported on slender iron posts. When I was there the building was enlivened by ornate papier-mâché chickens suspended from the ceiling, left over from the Abergavenny Food Fair, one of the annual events that takes place here.

Abergavenny
Town Hall.

In medieval times the market stalls were in what is now Nevill Street, a little further west, but by the seventeenth-century markets were held in an earlier building on the present site. Abergavenny still has its weekly cattle market, which is held on Tuesdays on land that was once the town's cricket pitch. However, Monmouthshire County Council plans to redevelop the site as a retail park including a large supermarket, with the cattle market relocated at Bryngwyn, near Raglan.

GRACED BY ROYALTY
ABERGAVENNY TITHE BARN

In the shadow of St Mary's Church in the centre of the town is the historic Tithe Barn, now restored to community use after a rather chequered recent history.

This thirteenth-century building, believed to be the oldest such barn in Wales, had been in danger of collapse when the parish sold it for £400 in 1948. It survived more or less intact, but in the intervening years, during which it had various uses including a storeroom and a carpet shop, it became very down-at-heel and something of an embarrassment.

By the late 1990s, when the barn was up for sale once more, St Mary's Church had a vision for its future use at the heart of the community. It was about to be sold to a private bidder but the vicar, Canon Jeremy Winston, was given three weeks to find the £100,000 to buy it back. An urgent appeal was launched and the response, in the form of gifts and loans from the people of Abergavenny, meant that he was able to raise the money.

The Prince of Wales visiting the Tithe Barn, Abergavenny, October 2008. (© Peter Dash)

A Development Trust was set up to oversee a Millennium Project to develop the building as a centre for exhibitions, education and hospitality. The Prince of Wales agreed to become the Trust's Patron and attended the service in St Mary's that launched the project.

In October 2008 he was back again to mark the completion of the project. A Service of Thanksgiving was held in St Mary's and Prince Charles then toured the barn's facilities. The ground floor is occupied by the Taste of Wales café where he enjoyed a cup of tea and a slice of bara brith. Upstairs there is a museum whose state-of-the-art exhibits explore 1,000 years of Abergavenny's history and which were designed to appeal to children and adults alike, as well as a commemorative tapestry, the work of some sixty local stitchers.

'From the beginning the day was one of the happiest parish occasions,' Canon Winston told the Monmouth Diocesan magazine. 'The rain left off and, from the moment of his arrival until His Royal Highness left, there was a great sense of celebration. One highlight was his keen interest in the activities of the children from local schools.'

VENERABLE YEWS AND AN ANCIENT ROOD
BETTWS NEWYDD CHURCH

Ancient yews are found in many of our churchyards but not many places have three of them all over 1,000 years old. At Bettws Newydd, a few miles north of Usk, there are three specimens, each with a girth of over 20ft.

The largest is no less than 30ft round. It is possibly the oldest living thing in Monmouthshire, estimated to be over 2,000 years old. It is still thriving – visitors who peer into its hollow centre will see a new stem growing inside. The yew growing by the churchyard wall shows a later stage in this natural regeneration process. The lower branches, having reached down to the ground, have put down roots themselves. Each one forms an independent tree.

The third specimen, found behind the church, also has a hollow trunk. This is not the symptom of decay that it might appear – hollow trees are actually less at risk from high winds.

The oldest churchyard yews date back to ancient times and pagan worship. These beliefs survived in the old custom of mourners tucking a sprig of yew into the shroud of the deceased and laying branches beneath the coffin. Christianity used the yew tree's evergreen leaves and remarkable powers of regeneration as a symbol of the Resurrection. Yew boughs were often used in Palm Sunday processions. It was also said that yew made the best longbows! Yew was an antidote to adder bites and today is used in the manufacture of drugs used to treat cancer patients.

The yews alone would be sufficient reason to seek out Bettws Newydd, but the church itself is an architectural gem. Its chief glory is the magnificent fifteenth-century rood loft that dominates this tiny building. The puritan excesses of the sixteenth century saw the destruction of similar structures almost everywhere – Bettws Newydd's is the most complete survival. Simon Jenkins writes that it has 'a rough self-confidence, as if made by local carpenters and with pride'. A much-restored example can be seen seven miles away at Llangwm Uchaf. Other features of great age at Bettws Newydd include a Norman font, the thirteenth-century west door and the base of a preaching cross on the south side of the church.

It is also worth finding All Saints' Church, Kemeys Commander. This tiny church lies down a farm lane off the road between Usk and Abergavenny. It too has a screen but no rood loft. There is a timber-framed entrance porch at the west end. The oversize double bell-cote is poised somewhat threateningly immediately above – even more alarming when you look at the cracks on the wall inside the church!

Above left: The medieval rood screen at Bettwys Newydd.

Above right: All Saints' Church, Kemeys Commander.

An engraving of Clytha Castle by Sir Richard Hoare, Bt, in Archdeacon Coxe's *Historical Tour of Monmouthshire*.

MOURNING 'A MOST EXCELLENT WIFE'

CLYTHA CASTLE

Clytha Castle, sited on a prominent hilltop three miles west of Raglan, seems a cheery gothick folly in a spectacular setting, but owes its origin to a time of great sadness.

It was constructed in 1790 by William Jones of Clytha Park as a banqueting house. A plaque on the exterior tells us that it was built for 'the purpose of relieving a mind sincerely afflicted by the loss of a most excellent wife.' The architect was long-believed to be John Nash but, according to Newman, 'recently-discovered building accounts' show that it was designed by John Davenport.

It is a fairy-tale sham castle with massive, impractical arrow-slits prominently displayed, clearly designed to be observed from a distance. Loudon, an art historian quoted by Simon Jenkins, dismissed it as 'gaudily and affectedly common'.

The house is now the property of the Landmark Trust (from whom it can be rented) but can be seen from the park which is in the care of the National Trust.

Also within the parish are three architecturally-interesting farmhouses, Chapel Farm, Whitehouse Farm and Great House, all dating from the sixteenth century and retaining many original features.

THE RETURN OF THE TRUE CROSS
CWMYOY

The tiny village of Cwmyoy lies in the secluded valley of the Honddu in the Black Mountains. Its glory is its 700-year-old church which, owing to the unstable nature of the slope it is built on, seems to have shifted on its foundations so that no part of it is at right-angles to any other. Buttresses, beams and struts abound.

Simon Jenkins describes the result graphically:

> The tower tilts downhill at an angle that makes Pisa seem upright. In the churchyard headstone tumble in all directions, as if some calamity had upset the dead. Inside the church visitors might be on the deck of a galleon in a storm, with the chancel about to slide overboard.

The church possesses a rare treasure – a carved rood or crucifixion scene bearing a primitive relief of Christ wearing a crown. This is unique and stood for many years in a dusty corner of the tower, more or less forgotten about. It had been dug up in 1861 just outside the churchyard wall by a Mr Meredith of Cwmyoy Farm. The vicar at the time did not want it in the church and it had been placed in the farmhouse garden. It was in 1935 that Mr Meredith's son, by now aged seventy-eight, told of his father's discovery and only then was it restored to St Martin's. In 1957 the cross was stolen. The theft apparently took place some time between Easter and mid-May – and it was not missed until a scholarly visitor reported its absence.

Above left: St Martin's Church, Cwmyoy.

Above right: The medieval rood screen at Cwmyoy.

Somehow it had found its way to a London antique dealer's, via shady dealings in a Somerset pub, allegedly, and was only traced because an unsuspecting buyer asked experts from the British Museum to authenticate it! Now returned home – and well-secured – the cross, described in *The Buildings of Wales* as 'poignant, if quite crudely carved', can once more be seen at Cwmyoy.

Getting to the church by car can be quite a challenge. The lanes are steep and narrow and there is no obvious place to park when you get there. However, once you are at the gate of the churchyard, you will find a path whose stones are inscribed in sequence to read 'This path was laid in memory of Mark Gibbons, 5.5.1965 to 16.9.2000. Loved by all and a friend to everyone', a delightful and practical tribute. His burial place is marked, not by a modern mass-produced gravestone, but an old stone gatepost.

Inside the church, a memorial dated 1682 has an equally touching tribute. A verse, but not set out as such by the local craftsman: 'Thomas Price he takes his nap in our common mother's lap, waiting to hear the bridegroom say awake my dear and come away.'

Photographing the church's eccentric profile is also difficult. The best view, included in some old books, is now obscured by a large laurel bush that has grown up in recent years and it is necessary to climb the steep overgrown slope on the north side to get a reasonable vantage point.

THE STRANGE LIFE OF JOHN OF KENT
GROSMONT CHURCH

A legendary figure in the remote borderlands of Monmouthshire and Herefordshire is John of Kent. Archdeacon Coxe wrote in 1801 that:

> Grosmont rings with his achievements. Old and young women, men and boys, unite in relating with extreme volubility and without the smallest disagreements a series of extraordinary tales concerning this wonderful personage. Like Doctor Faustus, he is said to have made a pact with the Devil; but more successful than the Doctor, he evaded the conditions of the covenant and outwitted the Prince of Darkness, both in his life and at his death.

Even as a boy, it was said that he could make all the crows, that he was supposed to be stopping from feeding on the corn in the fields, fly into a roofless barn and remain there while he went to enjoy the delights of Grosmont Fair. The bridge over the Monnow, leading to Kentchurch, is still called John of Kent's Bridge and the story was that he had commanded the spirits that served him to construct it in just one night!

Who he really was is something of a mystery. Some said that he was a monk, university-educated and remarkable for his erudition; others that he was a close companion of the great Owain Glendwr himself, even his wizard. Coxe stated that visitors to Kentchurch Court, just over the border in Herefordshire, were shown the stable where he kept his horses 'on which he traversed the air'. A portrait of him, which Coxe saw and reproduced in his book, is still kept at Kentchurch.

Even today John of Kent remains an enigma. He was the subject of an investigation by Alex Gibbon, published in 2004. *The Mystery of Jack of Kent and the Fate of Owain Glendwr* combined history and folklore in a style that would appeal to devotees of *The Da Vinci Code*.

He died in 1348 and an old tombstone in Grosmont churchyard, close to the east wall of the chancel, was believed to cover his body. Under the terms of his deal with the Devil, his soul would become the property of Satan should he be buried either inside or outside the church. Cunningly, John stipulated that he should be interred under the wall so that he was neither inside nor outside, thus saving his soul! Coxe writes that 'at the time of both my visits to Grosmont, this tomb was covered with a quantity of rubbish which prevented me from inspecting it.'

Grosmont church is large and imposing, like that at Trellech, a reminder of the days when the place was a town of considerably more importance than it is today. Entering it is quite a shock for the visitor as the nave is largely disused, services taking place beyond a glass partition put up in 1888. What remains is a vast space like the Great Hall of Winchester Castle. Stacks of old chairs are piled up on one side. If John of Kent had been buried under these even the Devil himself would have had a job finding him!

An engraving of John of Kent by Sir Richard Hoare, Bt, based on a portrait seen by Archdeacon Coxe at Kentchurch Court.

IMPORTANT MARKET TOWN,
LONG AGO FALLEN ON HARD TIMES

GROSMONT

In its quiet streets it is hard to believe it now but Grosmont was once a major border garrison town and market centre. Archdeacon Coxe wrote that it had been 'a place of considerable importance and is still governed by a mayor and burgesses'. He went on to describe how 'the natives boast of its former extent, point out spots at some distance which had formed streets of the town and allude to a tradition that once a market was held'.

Grosmont's decline had been going on for a long time by 1801. Way back in 1563 a survey quoted by Newman reported that 'tymber, iron and lead is rotten or taken away'. Newman goes on to describe Grosmont today: 'A close intricate village climbing up the hill – but the Town Hall, which encroaches on the road half-way up, tells that it is more than a village.'

The Town Hall that we see today is a somewhat curious rebuild, dating from 1832 and paid for by the Duke of Beaufort, the Lord of the Manor. The council chamber on the first floor is reached by an external stone stairway. At ground-floor level is an open arcaded market space in which stands the octagonal top step of the late medieval churchyard cross, which has somehow ended up in here. When I visited, this area was incongruously furnished with old armchairs and a television set was precariously balanced on the remains of the cross base. It seemed a somewhat disrespectful way to treat an ancient historical relic!

Grosmont's castle is reached up an inconspicuous side-turning off the village street. Much of what can be seen was the work of feudal baron Hubert de Burgh. It is thought that it dates from after 1219 when his campaigning in France introduced him to the latest thinking in castle design. In 1227 the king granted him 'fifty oaks for his new works at Grosmont'.

Unlikely furnishings at Grosmont Town Hall.

During Henry III's reign, according to Coxe quoting an earlier writer called Lombarde, when the castle was being attacked by the Welsh Prince Llewellyn, 'the king came with a great army to raise the siege, wherof some of the Welshmen had understandinge, they saved their lives with their legges' – which I take to mean that they ran away!

However, in a subsequent engagement, Henry found that 'his provisions were cut off and, being unable to prosecute his intended enterprise, he retreated to Grosmont and camped in the vicinity of the castle. During the night a large party of the enemy's horse surprised the king's troops asleep in the trenches and carried away 500 horses, with many wagons, baggages, provisions and much treasure'. The last time Grosmont Castle saw significant action was in 1405 when the Welsh under Glendwr, attacked it without success.

Town Farm, close to the Town Hall, is a largely unaltered house dating from 1673 and across the lane is a barn which has 1671 on the door lintel. There are other unspoiled traditional farmhouses of similar date in the district.

RESTORED WINDMILL
LLANCAYO

Llancayo Windmill beside the B4598 a couple of miles north of Usk, has recently been restored after lying derelict for 180 years. It was built in 1813 by Edward Berry, a retired mariner who took up agriculture after years of being at sea.

With its tall tapering stone tower and sweeping sails, it must have been prominent in the landscape of the Vale of Usk but it operated for just a few years before being burnt out in a fire in around 1830.

Llancayo Windmill.

Restoration work began in 2006, being undertaken by local property developer Peter Morgan whose wife, Helen, used to play around the mill as a child, when it was owned by his grandfather. 'It was a great opportunity to bring the land back into the family,' Mr Morgan told the *South Wales Argus* in July 2009.

The stonework was mostly still in good condition, despite the years of neglect, but it was necessary to render this with a historically accurate mix containing horsehair. New internal timbers and ironwork were needed. The sails operate on windy days but a generator is needed to power the mill at other times. The mill is not open to the public but can be hired as a holiday let.

SGRAFFITO BENEDICITE
LLANFAIR KILGEDDIN

Do not look for Llanfair Kilgeddin church in the village of the same name because you will not find it there. It is over a mile away to the north-east, close to the river and reached along a narrow lane off the B4598 between Abergavenny and Usk. Simon Jenkins described it as sitting 'forlorn in a field overgrown with grass, a scatter of tombstones nearly consumed by vegetation'. Someone must have taken these words to heart because when I visited in September 2009 the church was approached across a vast swathe of neatly mown municipal greensward. I think I would have preferred a more atmospheric overgrown churchyard!

The church was energetically restored by the architect J.D. Seddon in 1873, working for the vicar, Revd W.J. Coussmaker Lindsay, who was clearly a man who did not do things by halves. Sadly, ten years later, his wife Rosamund Lindsay died. He decided to beautify the interior in her memory and commissioned the artist Heywood Sumner to do the work.

Sumner had an impeccable pedigree. His father was the Bishop of Winchester and his mother had founded the Mothers' Union. He chose to illustrate the Benedicite, the hymn of praise from the *Book of Common Prayer*, in sgraffito panels. Sgraffito is a technique, Roman in origin, which uses thin layers of different coloured plaster cut back to reveal the required colour underneath.

The sixteen panels dominate the walls of the nave. Perhaps the finest is 'O Ye Mountains and Hills' which shows the Usk valley and the Sugar Loaf mountain. Another has a boy bowling a hoop and a little girl picking flowers, while a coastal scene features a rather comical walrus. Jenkins writes that 'each is a swirling composition of Art Nouveau lines, sometimes Pre-Raphaelite in appearance and sometimes startlingly modern'.

Unfortunately, 100 years later the church was in a sorry state. Experts consulted by the Church Council advised that a large sum of money would be needed for essential repairs, far more than the scattered community could afford. The church was declared redundant and closed.

Above: 'O Ye Mountains and Hills'.
A sgraffito panel by Heywood
Summer, Llanfair Kilgeddin.

Left: Crawshay family gravestones,
Llanfair Kilgeddin churchyard.

It was taken on by the Friends of Friendless Churches, a national organisation
founded by Ivor Bulmer-Thomas in 1957 to save churches of historic and
architectural interest threatened by demolition or 'unseemly conversion'. Cadw
offered a 100 per cent grant to pay for the repairs and in June 1988 a service was
held in the church to celebrate the end of the restoration campaign, which had
in fact cost far less than the pessimistic estimates that had led to its closure. With
generous help from the Pilgrim Trust, the sgraffito panels were restored in 2006-7
in memory of Lord (Roy) Jenkins, who was born and brought up not far away at
Abersychan and Pontypool.

Perhaps because of its remote location, the church is only open occasionally,
but the panels can at least be glimpsed through the windows. Also of interest are
the group of gravestones commemorating members of the Crawshay iron-making
family, standing apart in military formation south west of the church.

CANAL-SIDE VILLAGE BENEATH WOODED SLOPES
LLANFOIST

Llanfoist today is almost a suburb of Abergavenny but it still has its character and has an impressive setting beneath the wooded slope of the Blorenge.

The church is noted for its associations with the pioneers of the iron industry, many of whom chose to live here, away from the sights and sounds of the commercial processes that made them their fortunes. It was restored in 1872 in memory of Crawshay Bailey, whose memorial obelisk is in the churchyard, but retains some older features. There is a medieval cross, unusually complete except for the loss of its head. In the porch is what Arthur Mee described in 1951 as 'a broken stone with a carved relief of a pious, plain-faced lady of the seventeenth century, wearing a long skirt, tight bodice with puffed sleeves, a big ruff and shoes tied with tiny bows ... beside her is a big shovel'. I wonder who she was – and what was the significance of the shovel?

Llanfoist House, once the home of Crawshay Bailey, is an austere eighteenth-century house, beautifully situated below the slopes of the Blorenge Mountain, one of the hills that gives Abergavenny such a magnificent setting.

The Brecon & Abergavenny Canal runs through attractive mature woodland along the foot of the Blorenge. In 1822 a tramroad was built from the ironworks at Blaenavon to link with the canal at Llanfoist. The remains of three steep inclined planes can be seen, also the ruins of the incline's drum and brakehouse and stables. At the bottom of the incline the Wharfinger's house of 1822 still stands beside the canal, facing the loading dock. On the north side of the canal dock is a boathouse, which was originally used as a warehouse, built to store iron products from Blaenavon. Newman describes this as 'one of the earliest railway warehouses anywhere'.

Wharfinger's House, Llanfoist Wharf.

Llanfoist was on the London & North Western Railway's Heads of the Valleys line from Abergavenny to Merthyr and from here there is a dramatic walk along the old track, now a footpath, as it climbs high above the Clydach Gorge on its way to Brynmawr.

'THAT'S THE ONE I DON'T GO TO'
LLANGWM

'The church is located at the end of a farm track on the sloping banks of a stream', writes Simon Jenkins, advising architecture pilgrims in search of St Jerome's, Llangwm Uchaf. 'It should not be confused with another church passed on the same track.' In truth, the word 'track' makes it sound worse than it really is – narrow certainly, but properly surfaced, more a lane than a track.

Following his instructions, I went past the unregarded church of Llangwm Isaf and, after nearly heading straight on up someone's private drive, I turned sharply to the right and on to St Jerome's.

It is well worth finding. Its secluded position, down a slope from the lane, and its rugged tower, are reminiscent of deepest Devon. Inside is an ancient screen, more heavily-restored than that at Bettws Newydd but massively impressive. 'The composition is grand for so small a space,' Jenkins observes, 'as if awaiting the arrival of the enveloping woods to creep in and colonise it.'

This evocative image is appropriate because lurking on pillars beyond can be seen three faces of 'green men', those almost pagan fertility symbols with greenery sprouting from their mouths. Another curious object, found during restoration work and now positioned near the door, seems to be part of a pillar with a bowl

A 'green man' on a pillar in the chancel of St Jerome's Church, Llangwm.

shape scooped out of the top. It is decorated with an interlaced trellis design. It is thought to be Saxon, but whether it is a holy water stoup, an oil lamp or a piscina, no one seems to know.

St Jerome's has attracted visitors for many years. The way there is marked by hand-painted brown signposts, themselves now of some antiquity. Feeling sorry for the humble little church that we had been advised to ignore, I stopped at Llangwm Isaf on the way back. Its churchyard was neatly tended but the interior was rather sad. An aura of damp and bat-droppings testified to the difficulty of maintaining two ancient rural churches in such close proximity. Walking round outside I observed a broken window, cracked stonework and a door that was slowly disintegrating.

No one knows why Llangwm has two churches, both of them well away from the village itself. A leaflet in St Jerome's speaks vaguely of 'monastic influence' but I wonder whether some now-forgotten row split the congregation there centuries ago. Such things are not unknown in South Wales. I remember the old joke about the shipwrecked Welshman who built two chapels on his desert island. When rescued, he was asked why he had built two. 'You see that one on the left?' he replied. 'That's the one I don't go to.'

BIG BEN'S INSPIRATION AND A GUARDIAN OF WELSH IDENTITY
LLANOVER

Llanover, between Abergavenny and Pontypool, is a charming estate village that owes its origins to the patronage of Sir Benjamin Hall (who eventually was ennobled as Baron Llanover of Llanover and Abercarn) and his wife Augusta. She is nationally-known and honoured in Wales, while he is remembered, if at all, in England as the man after whom Big Ben, symbol of London and the Mother of Parliaments the world over, is named – though to be strictly accurate, of course, 'Big Ben' refers to the great bell, not the clock tower in which it is housed.

Benjamin Hall first became prominent in public life as a man who successfully challenged the powerful Somerset family, in whose pocket the House of Commons seat for the Monmouthshire Boroughs had been secure in the days before the Great Reform Act of 1832. He went on to have a distinguished career in Parliament, culminating in being First Commissioner of Works from 1855 to 1858.

Throughout his career he continued to champion Welsh causes. He supported John Frost and the Chartists in Newport and elsewhere, although he disapproved of their use of violence in support of a just cause. He was an early champion of the Welsh language, especially in public worship, and had Welsh churches built on his considerable estates, as at Abercarn. Having visited the philanthropic Scots industrialist Robert Owen at his mills at New Lanark, he was keen to see that his own employees were well treated.

It was this philosophy that inspired the establishment of the 'model village' at Llanover. Unlike similar ventures elsewhere, it was not a densely-packed planned settlement so much as loose groupings of attractively-designed cottages over quite an extensive area. The link between the 'big house' and the tenants was an essential feature of life at Llanover and this was very much Augusta's responsibility. Traditional Welsh customs were encouraged and Christmas entertainments provided for the villagers were on a lavish scale. Throughout the year Sir Benjamin and his formidable wife offered prizes for the best-kept houses and farms, sheep and garden produce. They were greatly loved.

When the new bell-tower at the Houses of Parliament was under construction it seemed appropriate that the bell should be named in honour of the President of the Board of Works himself. The *Illustrated London News* reported in March 1856 that 'all the bells are, we believe, to be christened before they begin to ring. It is proposed to call our King of Bells 'Big Ben' in honour of Sir Benjamin Hall, during whose tenure of office it was cast'.

The traditional national costume (invented by Lady Llanover) as seen outside the Welsh gift shop in Newport.

In 2009, to mark the 150th anniversary of the completion of the clock tower at Westminster, pupils at Llanover primary school worked with Ned Heywood, a local ceramics artist, to design a plaque to commemorate Sir Benjamin. As well as a picture of him, the plaque includes panels representing aspects of his career. The completed plaque was presented to the Palace of Westminster where it is now on display.

Sir Benjamin Hall died in 1867 and is buried at Llanover. Augusta survived him by nearly thirty years and it is to her that much of the credit for the revival of interest in Welsh culture belongs. With her colleague Lady Charlotte Guest she undertook the daunting task of translating the *Mabinogion*, the famous collection of Welsh legends that became the inspiration for the Eisteddfod movement. She promoted competitions for recitation in Welsh and the playing of the harp. Many things now regarded as typically Welsh stem from her. The so-called 'Welsh national costume' of tall black hat and red shawl is said to owe more to her than to what was in fact traditionally worn by the rural poor! I wonder what this prim and proper Victorian lady would have made of the decidedly skimpy bedroom version of the costume that I saw recently in a shop window in Crane Street, Pontypool. A total abstainer, she ensured that there would be no places of alcoholic refreshment on the Llanover lands. Those that existed before were converted into tea shops and the pubs that remain in the area are just outside the estate boundaries.

The massive stone sarcophagus in the churchyard, erected for Augusta (who died in 1896, aged ninety-four) her husband and her father, is ornamented with heraldry, biblical texts and inscriptions, fittingly enough in both Welsh and English. The picturesque church stands isolated in fields close to the River Usk, some distance from the village. Near Rhyd-y-Meirch is another memorial, the Welsh Calvinist Methodist chapel, provided in 1898 under the terms of her will.

Many of the cottages that make Llanover such a delightful place in fact derive from the early twentieth century, designed in Arts & Crafts style by Alfred H. Powell for Lord Treowen. The inscription on the schoolhouse reads 'Ysgol, Harddwch, Gwlad', meaning 'Schooling, Beauty, Country'. At the time of writing, this school is threatened with closure by Monmouthshire Council due to falling pupil numbers.

VISIONS OF THE VIRGIN

CAPEL-Y-FFIN, LLANTHONY

Joseph Leycester Lyne was an eccentric priest of extreme High Church persuasion who believed he had a calling to restore the glories of medieval Benedictine monasticism to Britain. Known as Father Ignatius, he had already set up a short-lived religious community at Laleham in Middlesex, when in 1869 he came to Monmouthshire and built a monastery at Capel-y-Ffin, four miles further up the valley than the original Llanthony Abbey.

The regime was Romanist and austere. During Lent the buildings echoed to the sound of the Seven Dolours of the Holy Virgin rung on the great bell at set hours through the night. Marian devotion was the mainstay of the community's life.

On Monday, 30 August 1880, a Brother Dunstan was keeping watch over the Blessed Sacrament when he saw a blue mist over the tabernacle and the monstrance (the vessel containing the consecrated elements) shining through it. The nun taking the next watch saw the same thing, although Dunstan had not told her what he had experienced.

Cautiously, Father Ignatius advised them not to tell anyone else but the strange happenings continued. That evening one of the choirboys who had been playing football after Vespers came rushing, calling to Ignatius, 'Father, we have seen such a beautiful spirit in the meadow.' The other boys confirmed the story and Ignatius was now convinced that something deeply spiritual was happening.

'The eldest boy, who was about fifteen, said he was certain that what they had seen was the Blessed Virgin Mary,' he wrote:

> He saw a bright light over the hedge and the figure of a woman, with hands upraised as if in blessing and with a veil over her face, coming to him. She passed close enough for him even to see the material of the garments that she wore. The figure stood in a bright light in a bush that was illuminated with phosphorescent light. All the boys saw and described the same experience.

The former monastery at Capel-y-ffin.

On the night of 4 September the boys saw the burning bush again. They called the Brothers and, when they began to sing an Ave Maria, they saw the figure sending out rays of light. There was now a second figure – a man wearing a loincloth, his hands stretched out towards them.

The night of 15 September was close and muggy with the surrounding hills indistinct through the mist. As they sang the Hail Mary's, Father Ignatius saw:

> … a great circle of light flash out over the whole heavens, taking in the mountains, the trees, the ruined house and the monastery. From that one great circle of light, small circles bulged out and in the centre of the circles stood a gigantic figure with hands uplifted. I saw distinctly the outlines of the features against the bright light and also the exact form of the drapery from the sleeves of the upraised arms.

There were no more visions after that and when Father Ignatius spoke about what they had all seen, he was met with ridicule and suggestions of religious mania. He was, however, convinced that what they had experienced was a sign from God for the Church of England. If it was indeed a sign, it was a somewhat misleading one. By 1908 Ignatius was dead and the community down to three impoverished monks. The Church authorities were rather embarrassed by all the hysteria and refused to give them any support. The monastery building can still be seen across the field and every year devotees of Father Ignatius and his Order conduct a service of commemoration.

A strange postscript – Alan Roderick in his book *Haunted Gwent* also tells the story of a man driving towards Hay-on-Wye over the Gospel Pass seeing the figure of a man standing in the middle of the road and flagging him down. He was dressed in the habit of a Benedictine monk – but vanished as quickly as he had appeared!

'A RECLUSE SPOT SURROUNDED BY HILLS'
SKENFRITH

Archdeacon Coxe was uncharacteristically grumpy about Skenfrith, describing it as 'a miserable village, containing a church, a few cottages and two public houses and only remarkable for its castle, placed in a recluse spot surrounded by hills, on the margins of the limpid and murmuring Monnow.'

Maybe he was put off by the difficulties he had in getting there. He wrote that it was:

> … seldom visited by travellers as the access to it is difficult for carriages and horses. The road is scarcely passable although it is part of the turnpike to Ross. It leaves the carriage road about four miles from Monmouth and,

after traversing St Maughan's Common, proceeds through a narrow, steep and boggy lane, overgrown with thickets and pitched with large stones placed edgeways in the boggy soil. These stones being broken or displaced, a succession of steps is formed and horses not accustomed to such rugged and miry ways are apt to stumble and flounder.

No wonder Coxe was fed up when he got there.

The narrow lane through Maypole and St Maughan's is still there but the main road to Skenfrith from the south is the B4347 via Newcastle, passing the grand-looking house at Hilston Park.

In contrast to Coxe, Arthur Mee liked Skenfrith, as I did. He calls it 'one of the most attractive of all the Monmouthshire villages, with cottages, church and castle clustered together in complete harmony.'

The setting of the castle, overlooked by a wooded hillside is delightful. Archaeologists have seen traces of a twelfth-century building but what we see now dates from the early thirteenth. It has one of the oldest circular keeps in Wales, standing 40ft high on the partly-levelled motte of the earlier wooden keep.

However, the most stunning treasure is in the church. The Skenfrith Cope hangs, as it has since a refurbishment of the church in 1910, in a glass-fronted case at the east end of the north aisle. There are curtains drawn across to protect it from the effects of the light but pull these back and its glory is revealed. Made about 1500, this magnificent vestment worn by the priest at Mass, is deep red velvet and embroidered with figures of saints. The hood shows Mary and the baby

The Skenfrith Cope.

Jesus. There are many legends about the history of the Cope but all that is known for certain is that when Father Thomas Abbot, a Catholic priest from Monmouth, visited Skenfrith in the mid-nineteenth century, he found it being used as a cover for the Altar. The Cope deserves detailed examination – but please remember to close the curtains afterwards!

I am amazed that such a treasure is still kept in the church, which is usually left open for visitors. They are obviously a trusting lot in Skenfrith. Also in the north aisle, I found a stall with a tempting array of home-made cakes for sale, unattended with just a large bottle to leave the money in. I can recommend the Welsh Cakes and the almond tart!

The church largely escaped the attentions of the Victorian restorers and still has some old pews and other original fittings. The tomb-chest of John Morgan in the north aisle (died 1557) is a real gem. Sir John is portrayed as a bearded figure with wide-open eyes. He is dressed in an embroidered robe while his wife wears a gown with high puffed sleeves and a tight-fitting bodice girdled by a cord with dangling tassels. In panels on the front are his four sons, also shown bearded and elegantly dressed, as are his four daughters. The Morgans were clearly fashion-conscious!

Outside the church again, have a look at the tower. It looks as though it was intended to go higher but was prevented by the unstable foundations. A massive stone buttress was needed. At the top of the truncated tower there is a medieval timber belfry.

Next to the main road is the mill; once owned with the castle, it was later acquired by the Hilston Estate. It was driven by an undershot wheel, the water being led off the River Monnow by a leat. The mill was working until 1995.

MONMOUTHSHIRE'S MOST HAUNTED?

THE SKIRRID INN

The Skirrid Inn at Llanfihangel Crucorney near Abergavenny has made quite a name for itself as Monmouthshire's Most Haunted – allegedly!

Its reputation derives from its time as a courthouse and a hangman's noose is one of the relics that visitors are shown. The story goes that around 180 unfortunates were condemned to death there in the time of the notorious Judge Jeffries.

A more recent spectre is that of Fanny Price, wife of a former landlord. She, it is said, has been seen sitting in a wicker chair in an upstairs room but as soon as she is spotted, she vanishes! Whether any of the stories are true, it is impossible to say – but they are certainly good for business. The place is fully booked every Halloween!

Skirrid Mountain itself is to the south, back towards Abergavenny, in the angle between the A465 and the B4521. It is a popular destination for energetic walkers but those who suffer from vertigo should take note of the experience of Archdeacon Coxe when he visited the area on his tour of Monmouthshire in 1799.

Skirrid Mountain.

He was having a busy day – he had already climbed the Sugar Loaf in the morning in the company of a local guide but when they set out at two o'clock to climb the Skirrid, it soon became clear that this man was as lost as the intrepid Archdeacon. A farmer gave them directions, prefaced by something like 'but I wouldn't start from here'.

The climb was difficult and, in Coxe's words:

> … the heat was so intense, the fatigue which I had undergone in the day so considerable and the effort I impatiently made to reach the summit so violent that, when I looked down from the narrow ridge, the boundless expanse around and beneath which suddenly burst on my sight overcame me. I several times attempted to walk along the ridge but my head became so giddy as I looked down the precipitous sides that I could not remain standing. I seemed safe only when extended on the ground and was not therefore in a condition to examine the beauties of the view.

I know how he felt. Bravely, Coxe did return to Skirrid Mountain on another occasion and, ascending by an easier route from Llandewi Skirrid, he was able to appreciate the view which extends from Hereford Cathedral all the way round to the hills of Gloucestershire and Somerset. At the northern end of the ridge, its highest point, is the site of a medieval chapel. Coxe wrote that he 'could observe no traces either of walls or foundations' but he described two upright stones marking the entrance and covered in graffiti (nothing changes!). One inscription read 'Turner, 1671'.

'To this place many Roman Catholics are said to repair on Michaelmas Eve to perform their devotions,' he recorded. 'According to legend, the mountain was split asunder by an earthquake at the Crucifixion of Our Lord. The earth of this spot is considered sacred and was formerly carried away to cure diseases and to sprinkle on coffins; but whether this superstitious practice still continues, I was not able to ascertain.'

MEMORIAL TO A ROMAN SOLDIER
TREDUNNOCK CHURCH

Set in quiet country south of Usk, Tredunnock Church is approached through white-painted gates that were set up to mark the accession of King Edward VII in 1902. In the churchyard is the tomb of the daughter of the tragic Sir John Franklin, discoverer of the North West Passage in the Arctic north of Canada. Eleanor Isabella Gell died in 1860 of a disease through which she had heroically nursed a sick child.

The church was locked when I visited so I was not able to see its most notable monument: a sandstone memorial to a Roman soldier who died in about 100 AD. Arthur Mee translates its Latin inscription as follows:

To the memory of Julius Julianus, soldier of the Second Augustan Legion. He served eighteen years and lived forty years. He is buried here. Set up under the direction of his wife Amanda.

1902 gates, Tredunnock.

This stone had been attached to the outer wall of the church in antiquity and was unearthed by the sexton when digging a grave in about 1680. It is thought to have come from the Roman cemetery at Caerleon but how and why it found its way to Tredunnock is anybody's guess.

The name Newbridge nearly always actually means that an old one can be found there. At the Newbridge half a mile east of Tredunnock is a three-arch stone bridge dating from 1779 spanning the River Usk at the point where it ceases to be tidal. From here there is a fine view of the wooded slopes of Wentwood and it is hard to believe that you are only about a mile away from the roaring traffic on the dual-carriageway A449.

MARTYR'S GRAVE AND A QUIRKY CASTLE
USK

Near the west door of St Mary's Church is the grave of St David Lewis, the Catholic martyr (*see* Abergavenny, p.25 and Llantarnam, p.96). A plaque by the river, just upstream of the town bridge, marks the site of his martyrdom.

St Mary's nave, north aisle and tower are the remains of the Benedictine nunnery founded by Richard de Clare in the 1170s. By the entrance to the churchyard is the sixteenth-century Priory Gatehouse. The Town Hall in New Market Street was originally built right at the end of that century, after the Earl of Pembroke had granted Usk a new site for a market in 1598. The original site of the market was Twyn Square, between the church and the castle. With inns and a pretty little clock tower, it remains the natural centre of the town.

In 1799 Archdeacon Coxe wrote that:

Usk is undoubtedly a place of great antiquity and was of considerable extent. According to the tradition of the natives, several places at some distance from the present houses were once considered within its precincts. Many ancient houses are in ruins and a considerable district is much dilapidated, exhibiting the appearance of having been sacked and recently quitted by an enemy.

It had certainly declined from its medieval heyday and even today Usk remains a compact little town, hardly grown beyond its old boundaries. There are a number of old houses and inns. Outside the Three Salmons is the bell used by visitors on horseback to summon the inn's servants.

Despite acknowledging that 'no castle in Monmouthshire has been subject to more frequent assaults,' Coxe was not very impressed with it, describing its ruins as 'neither magnificent nor highly interesting'. Yet it has a noble history, the first record of it dating from 1138 when it was seized by the Welsh from the Norman de Clare family. The Keep, the earliest stone structure on the site, was built by Richard

Ostler's Bell at the Three
Salmons Inn, Usk.

de Clare, known to history as 'Strongbow' after he recovered it in 1174. As seen today, the main castle dates from the time of William Marshal, who won de Clare's daughter by knocking the future King Richard I off his horse in a joust in 1189.

From the mid-eighteenth century, Usk Castle belonged to the Dukes of Beaufort. In 1899 it passed to the Addams-Williams family of Llangibby Castle, who began the process of conservation. It remains in private hands and is open to the public – but not immediately easy to get to. It stands to the north of Twyn Square on a hillside that is so thickly wooded that it is only visible in winter. It is reached by a little lane leading up from the eastern end of Castle Parade.

In contrast to the Archdeacon, Simon Jenkins loved it:

The pleasure of Usk lies in the present rather than the past. If ruins must be ruins let them be like this, as if playing a game with the surrounding rocks and enveloping vegetation … It is wild, unmanicured and idiosyncratic. Whereas a Cadw castle is scrubbed and tidy Usk respects the dishevelment of age … Visitors are asked to put a pebble in a basket ('we are told we must count numbers') and entrance money in a dish, the most casual and economical unmanned entry control I know.

White Castle.

DAYS OUT FOR RUDOLF HESS

WHITE CASTLE

With Grosmont and Skenfrith, White Castle, two miles north-west of Llandeilo Crossenny, makes up the so-called Three Castles of Overwent. All three came into the ownership of feudal baron Hubert de Burgh until he fell out of favour with the king and were, in Archdeacon Coxe's picturesque spelling, 'ingulphed' into the possession of the House of Lancaster.

White Castle is the largest and most remote of the three and commands panoramic views over the surrounding countryside. Its stone buildings date from a rebuilding that began in 1184 and it was kept in repair until the mid-fifteenth century. By the time of James I it was 'ruinous and in decay time out of mind'. In 1922 the castle passed into the hands of the State and, like many historic buildings in Wales, it is now looked after by Cadw.

Arthur Mee provides an interesting postscript to White Castle's history. Writing soon after the end of the Second World War, he described how its 'goat, goldfish and swans were fed by Britain's Enemy Visitor. For here walked Rudolf Hess on occasional outings from the mental home in Abergavenny.'

3

The Gwent
Levels

ROMAN VILLA UNEARTHED BY *TIME TEAM*
CAERWENT

Caerwent possesses the best-preserved stretch of Roman Wall in Wales. From the site of the former East Gate close to the Coach & Horses pub in the main street, it is possible to walk the whole length of the southern side of the former Venta Silurum, round to where the West Gate once stood. Apart from a modern housing estate to the east, there has been as yet very little building outside the Roman walls, so there are fine views across fields and woods to the hills southward which screen off the motorways to the Severn Crossings. The rest of the walls, on the north side, have mostly gone but it is easy to see where they once were.

Much of the town plan has been established by excavations at various times during the twentieth century. There are several Roman structures visible. There are the remains of some houses and shops on the corner of Pound Lane in the north-west quadrant of the town; the temple which is just off the main street in the centre of Caerwent and the forum/basilica complex nearby. All of these have detailed information boards alongside so that visitors can understand what they are seeing.

Archaeologist Phil Harding at the *Time Team* excavation at Caerwent, 2008.

In the summer of 2008 *Time Team* carried out a three-day dig, concentrating on an extensive area in the north-west corner and a smaller one across the road from the temple. Despite all the earlier excavations, these were areas that had not previously been looked at properly. Near the temple they found evidence for more shops, emphasising Venta Silurum's importance as a trading centre. On the main site a large villa was discovered. This would have had mosaic floors and painted wall-plaster and was clearly the home of someone of high status, a wealthy farmer or some civic dignitary. There was also evidence for a plunge pool from a bath-house. For the archaeologists the find of the dig was a fine carved bone or antler knife with a foldaway blade depicting two gladiators in combat.

Many of the Roman artefacts from Caerwent are now in museums elsewhere but there are still some to be seen in the village. The War Memorial is on a Roman base and a number of important memorials have been preserved in the church.

The Royal Naval Propellant Factory was situated a mile north of Caerwent. This was established during the Second World War for the manufacture of cordite. It consisted of a group of flat-roofed buildings, well away from each other, surrounded by grassy earth banks to absorb the blast if anything went horribly wrong. The base was served by a railway which branched off the main line near Severn Tunnel Junction. For obvious reasons steam engines used on the line had spark-arrestor chimneys and were not allowed on certain parts of the line where shunting the explosives wagons was done using capstans and cables. Although the base is no longer operational, the rails are still in place on much of the line whose bridge crosses the A48 near Caerwent.

THE BATTLE OF THE FLAGS, 2009
CALDICOT

A squabble that would have made an apt subject for one of those whimsical Ealing Comedy films divided Caldicot in 2009, making the town – in the words of the Mayor, David Evans – 'an object of ridicule'.

When the Town Council came under the control of Plaid Cymru councillors decided that the Welsh national flag, the Red Dragon, should fly from the flagpole at the Council's offices in Sandy Lane. In this community, which appears to be culturally more English than Welsh, not everyone approved. A campaign led by Chamber of Commerce Events Chairman, Mike Rice, eventually succeeded – in the face of bitter Plaid Cymru opposition – in getting a second flagpole erected for the Union Jack, 'to mark the efforts of British servicemen abroad'.

All was well until three months later when someone noticed that the English flagpole was slightly further up a slope and therefore eight inches higher than the Welsh one! Mr Rice, quoted in the *South Wales Argus*, said that 'the pole manufacturer stated that the Union Flag should be the higher of the two.'

Left: This picture of the headquarters of Caldicot Town Council was taken after the Union Jack had been stolen.

Below: The English on top!

Caldicot Town Council   Cyngor Tref Cil-y-Coed

Parking is permitted for visitors to Town Council only

Caniateir parcio i'r rhai sy'n ymweld â swyddfa Cyngor y Dref yn unig.

Vehicles parked at Owner's Risk
Bydd cerbydau'n cael eu parcio ar fenter eu perchnogion.

Plaid Cymru councillors, supported by one 'Independent', then pushed through a motion ordering the Chamber of Commerce, who paid for the second flagpole, to lower it at its own expense. On behalf of the Chamber, Mr Rice said that they would not do so until they saw 'an official document stating that they are wrong'.

Soon afterwards the Union Jack went missing! Town Hall officers reported the theft to the police. The flag was believed to have been taken sometime between 5 p.m. on Tuesday 19 May and 8 a.m. the next morning. Mr Rice was very angry and vowed that the flag would be replaced. 'I've talked to people in the village and they are disgusted,' he told the *Argus*. 'It is appalling that someone should do this.'

Bemused local residents might be forgiven for thinking that, in the middle of the worst economic recession since the 1930s, their elected representatives had more important matters to deal with!

Incidentally, the notice outside the Council Offices stating that parking there is reserved for councillors only has the English wording printed above the Welsh version. One wonders how long it will be before there are demands that this be changed.

ELEGANT ART DECO BATHROOM IN MEDIEVAL CASTLE
CALDICOT CASTLE

Caldicot seems to bring out the worst in people. In his 2009 book *Eleven Minutes Late: A Train Journey to the Soul of Britain*, Matthew Engel refers to his personal list of 'Britain's Vilest Towns'. 'The malevolently inhospitable dump of Caldicot' comes second! Despite the antics of its politicians, this seems a little unfair to me.

Hidden amid its Sixties housing estates, Caldicot has two medieval curiosities. One is its castle, which, after Chepstow and Raglan, is the largest and best-preserved in the county. However, it is somewhat inconspicuous; 'finding it requires an act of will', according to Simon Jenkins. In 1885 the decrepit remains were acquired by a wealthy benefactor, J.R.Cobb. It would seem that he was something of a collector of castles, having also acquired those at Manorbier and Pembroke in West Wales. It was the Cobb family who installed the somewhat unlikely Art Deco bath in one of the towers.

The castle is now owned by Monmouthshire Council. It is open to the public (at a reduced charge to Monmouthshire ratepayers) and events are held here throughout the year.

Llanthony Secunda Manor in Church Road is equally hard to find. It is a medieval house, modified in the seventeenth century, a private residence but available for photo-shoots and similar activities.

The Art Deco bath in Caldicot Castle.

THE GREAT FLOOD

GOLDCLIFF

It is easy to miss Goldcliff Church, which lies set back behind the Farmer's Arms pub on the road towards Nash. Dating from the thirteenth and fourteenth centuries and with a low tower, it is one of several on the Levels that bears witness to the Great Flood of 1606/7 (the variation in year being due to the later modification of the calendar).

The churchwardens in that momentous year put up a brass plaque on the north wall of the church, close to the altar. This plaque still survives, its archaic lettering and rustic attempt at describing the event in verse somehow being more vivid than a strictly accurate scientific account would be:

On the 20th day of January 1606, even as it came to pass, it pleased God the flud did flow to the edge of this same bras, and in this parish there was lost £5,000 in stock etc., besides 22 people was in this parish drowned.

Cynics might observe that the wardens seem to regard the loss of valuable animals to be of higher priority than the death of twenty-two people!

The flood memorial plaque in Goldcliff Church.

The cause of this devastating flood has been argued about ever since and was the subject of two programmes in the BBC2 *Timewatch* series in recent years. Scientists now believe that the giant wall of water that swept across the low lands on both sides of the Severn Estuary was triggered either by an earthquake under the Atlantic Ocean – a theory made topical by the Asian tsunami on Boxing Day 2004 – or a storm surge up the Bristol Channel. There is credible evidence for both theories.

In the more religious times back in the seventeenth century many saw it as a judgement from God. Puritan pamphleteers, angered by what they saw as the Anglican Church's increased tolerance of Catholicism, claimed that it was evidence of God's anger with the wickedness of the nation, in much the same way as some Islamic teachers saw the 2004 tsunami as just punishment for scantily-clad Western tourists being allowed on the beaches of Bali.

Linking the flood with an outbreak of plague in 1603 and the Gunpowder Plot of 1605, William Jones wrote in *God's Warning to His People of England* that:

> Many are the dombe warninges of destruction which the Almighty God hath lately scourged this our kingdome with; and many more are threatening tokens of his heavy wrath extended towards us; all which, in bleeding hearts may inforce us to put on the true garment of repentance ... Let us also call to remembraunce the most wicked and pretended malice of the late papisticall conspiracie of traytors; that with powder practised the subversion of this beautiful kingdome.

In *Lamentable Newes from Monmouthshire* another writer thundered that 'these prodigious overflowing of the waters proceed from the Lord's own direction. Speedy repentance and amendment doe avert his fearful wrath and judgement from us.'

With Global Warming, blamed on human greed and materialism, forecast to bring about rising sea levels, threatening the Gwent Levels with inundation once again, some might argue that he is quite right!

'HE ALSO DIED SERVING THE NATION'
LLANWERN

For many, the name Llanwern brings to mind the steelworks. The village of Llanwern is some distance away from the factory, sandwiched between the works and the Southern Distribution Road that marks the limit of the built-up area of Newport. It is actually far more attractive than this description would suggest, as Arthur Mee described it in 1951, 'a pretty tree-shaded village four miles east of Newport.' On the slope of Cot Hill is the sixteenth-century house called Great Milton, recently most attractively restored.

The church is a quarter of a mile from the village but significant lumps and bumps in the field across the road suggest that the settlement has been relocated, possibly to clear the area for the park of the long-gone 'big house'. The Georgian Llanwern House no longer exists but in the early twentieth century it was the home of David Alfred Thomas, who came from a family that made its money in the South Wales mining industry and who served in the First World War government.

In May 1915 he was on board the *Lusitania* with his daughter when the ship was torpedoed by the Germans with the loss of nearly 1,200 lives. Both survived and a few months later he was sent to organise the supply of munitions from the USA and Canada. For this work he was rewarded with a peerage as Baron Rhondda of Llanwern, later becoming Viscount.

He never forgot the village from which he took his title and he paid for the homely-looking Village Institute, designed in Arts & Crafts style by Oswald Milne, an architect he employed to work on Llanwern Park from about 1906. There are several houses of the same period in the village, notably Wisteria, Myrtle and Bay Tree Cottages.

Towards the end of the war Lord Rhondda was given the onerous task of stamping out the Black Market speculation and profiteering that was shaming the country at that time. He was responsible for the introduction of a fairer system of rationing. The strain of the job brought about his death in July 1918 at the age of sixty-two. He is buried in Llanwern churchyard, his grave marked by a tall obelisk. He is also commemorated on the War Memorial in the Square at Magor, a few miles away. On this unusual memorial, as well as the names of those who died in battle, is a plaque which reads 'Remember also David Alfred Thomas, 1st Viscount Rhondda, for he too died serving the nation as Food Controller.'

A pinnacle from the Houses of Parliament in Llanwern churchyard.

An equally curious, but much less ostentatious memorial can be found by the wall near the western edge of the churchyard. A small stone pinnacle, it bears a plaque certifying that it is a genuine piece of the Houses of Parliament and dates from the 1940s. How this relic found its way to Llanwern is a mystery.

GREAT WESTERN STATION LIVES ON ... JUST!
LLANWERN

There is no station now in Station Road, Llanwern, and has not been one since September 1960 when it was closed, just as work was starting on the huge Spencer Steelworks nearby. It was a curious decision – presumably it was assumed that all the workers at the new site would have cars.

The road led not only to the station but also on across the tracks to the villages of Goldcliff and Nash out on the Levels. However, this road was also closed as the works were to be built across it. The road network in the area still bears the scars of ruthless amputation to accommodate the steelworks.

Yet the old metal signpost still remains – with one arm painted out in black, pointing forlornly to 'Llanwern GWR station, Goldcliff, Nash'. Beyond the golf clubhouse, there are two rows of large, well-maintained houses, standing alongside another road that leads nowhere except a turning space for the little bus that is an important lifeline for some elderly residents here. Presumably these houses were originally put up because of the proximity of the station, enabling a convenient commute into Newport or Bristol.

Now no trains stop at Llanwern and the bus service seems permanently under threat of being withdrawn. Such is the march of progress!

Painted-out signpost, Llanwern.

MORE THAN JUST A SERVICE AREA
MAGOR

Many will only know Magor as the name of a Service Area on the M4 near Newport but it is worth taking the opposite direction at the roundabout and visiting the village itself. Considerably expanded in recent years and now very much a dormitory settlement for Newport and Bristol, Magor nevertheless still has a recognisable older centre with an impressive church, two old pubs, a post office and a square that is the hub of local life.

A feature of the square is the War Memorial. It is of unusual classical design and, as well as the names of those who died in conflict, also bears a tribute to Lord Rhondda, the First World War Food Controller who died in 1918 (*see* Llanwern, p.59).

Overlooking the car park to the west of the churchyard are the gaunt remains of what is known as The Procurator's House. Between 1238 and 1385, according to Newman, the tithes from Magor were collected by this official on behalf of the Italian abbey of Anagni. However, the house of which we see the cliff-like remains, probably dates from the sixteenth century when the vicar of Magor was a priest appointed by Tintern Abbey. At the end of the car park nearer the square there is an isolated gable end and stone fireplace from a different house that has long gone.

The adjacent villages of Magor and Undy have merged into one another, to the extent that not even local people can agree where the boundary lies. I have been told that people from Undy do not get on well with those from Magor, and vice versa. Some say that this goes back to the days when the villagers were on different sides in the Civil War!

Above left: The War Memorial at Magor.

Above right: The tribute to Lord Rhondda on Magor War Memorial.

Portskewett Church and Harold's Field.

TIME TEAM UNEARTHS KING HAROLD'S LODGE
PORTSKEWETT

The pretty little church at Portskewett stands beside the main road at the western end of the village. It overlooks a field whose lumps and bumps gave rise to the local belief that these were relics of a stronghold which Earl Harold had built in 1064 to protect the crossing of the Severn. The story was that the following year he entertained Edward the Confessor, who had been with his Court at Gloucester. Soon afterwards the place was burned down by a Welsh chieftain, Cradoc ap Griffith.

In 2007 the archaeologists from Channel Four's *Time Team* programme spent three days excavating in the field to test the truth of the legend. The site is a scheduled ancient monument and this was the first dig to be allowed there. It was a tall order to attempt to locate any remains of a timber structure which had been burned to the ground almost 1,000 years before!

Things got even more complicated when what they discovered under the largest mound were traces of a previously-unsuspected Norman manor house. That was interesting in itself but its construction had almost certainly destroyed any remains of Harold's timber building. However, one tiny piece of Saxon pottery was enough to convince the team that there was something in the tale of him building at Portskewett, though it seems likely it was a hunting lodge rather than a fortress.

Time Team presenter Tony Robinson, speaking to the *South Wales Argus*, said of the Saxon fragment 'it's not much, but finding this from a time when there simply was not much pottery feels like discovering the Holy Grail. We have found evidence of activity here just before the Norman Conquest and for me it's proof enough that Harold was here. Our historian is convinced that Harold would have built his hunting lodge on this important hill intending it to stand out as a symbol of new power to anyone arriving in the creek below.' However, Steve Clarke of the Monmouth Archaeological Society struck a note of caution. 'I believe it could be the site where Harold built his hunting lodge,' he said, 'but I would have liked more evidence.'

Portskewett Church, yellow-limewashed and, according to Arthur Mee, 'looking in the distance not unlike a cardboard model', stands in a neatly-maintained churchyard but sadly has been locked whenever I have tried to get inside. This end of the village has seen dramatic changes in recent years. There is a busy new industrial estate on the road towards Caldicot and the attractive gabled manor farmhouse stands unhappily in the middle of a building site. It dates from the sixteenth century and was altered in the mid-seventeenth when the parlour was given a handsome plaster ceiling. It is claimed that King Charles I spent a night here in 1645.

A STONE CIDER MILL AND PRESS
REDWICK

Visitors coming into Redwick from the direction of Magor are faced with what looks like a particularly fine stone-built bus shelter at the end of the road. In fact, it was designed by a local man, Hubert Jones, as a home for various agricultural relics salvaged from farmhouses in the village when they were being modernised and dates from about 1975.

The interior of the building is dominated by a large stone cider mill and press that came from The Bryn, not far away. There are mill wheels, an old fireback and a cast-iron notice relating to the activities of the drainage board. Nearby, but not under cover, are the village stocks. Perhaps it was felt that these might be brought back into use one day and that the miscreant deserved to be left out in the rain!

The ancient church has a fine tower which is a local landmark. There is a curious story concerning the bellringers here on New Year's Eve more than a century ago. It is said that they were whiling away the time until it was midnight by playing cards. The door of the ringing chamber suddenly flew open. One of the ringers went and shut it. A few minutes later the same thing happened again. This time he bolted it as well, just to make sure. When the door burst open for a third time the terrified men fled. They did not dare to ring the bells that night and vowed never to play cards in the church again.

It is a strange tale, not least because the ringers at Redwick nowadays stand, not in the ringing chamber but below, in the main body of the church. Perhaps they feel safer among the congregation! A plaque on the door to the Rood Loft lists those involved in the bellringing in the 1990s, not only the ringers but those who provided the refreshments – and quite right too.

An older notice records a bequest of land by parishioners John Quinton and his wife Mary to provide aid for the 'needy and impotent of the said parish'. There must later have been some dispute about the terms of this arrangement because an apologetic paragraph at the foot of the board reads 'The original deed dated 5 December 1696 and now in the parish church safe having been in former days mislaid; the present Vicar, Churchwardens and Overseers have caused this board to be erected AD 1886 that the benefaction to the parish may not be lost sight of'.

Another unusual feature of the church is the total-immersion font lurking behind a timber screen at the end of the south aisle. A feature of many Baptist chapels, such things are rarely found in Anglican churches, although the practice continued well beyond the Reformation. The faint-hearted might be relieved to know that there is also a more typical font which is used for baptisms nowadays. Redwick likes to provide items in duplicate – the church also has two 1607 flood marks. Somewhat confusingly, they show slightly different water levels.

The cider mill at Redwick.

'ROPING' – OR 'A RANSOM FOR THE BRIDE'

REDWICK

As Roy Palmer reports, the old wedding custom of 'Roping' and the payment of a ransom before the bride and groom are allowed to leave the churchyard survived in many parts of Monmouthshire.

A rope was tied across their path and not removed until coins for the children had been thrown by the bridegroom or the best man. A tradition first recorded at Itton near Chepstow in 1811, the details varied slightly from place to place. At Penallt four bouquets tied to the rope were detached after the payment of the ransom and given to bride, groom, best man and chief bridesmaid.

Roping is known to have been common practice during the early twentieth-century in Newport and the surrounding villages but has largely died out now. Palmer wrote (in 1998) that 'it continued at Devauden until the 1970s and is still kept up at Penallt.'

It still happens too at Redwick, where my younger daughter was married in August 2009. This was, in fact, maintaining a family tradition because we found the same custom at Compton Greenfield, north of Bristol, where my wife Linda and I were married in 1973. A variation there was that the gates of the lychgate were secured and not untied until the groom had lifted the bride over. I am afraid that I prevailed upon my best man to assist in this task, after the clergyman who married us told me the cautionary tale of an unfortunate young man who had slipped a disc – which cannot have done much for their wedding night!

The ransom having been paid, the bridegroom is allowed to cut the rope! (© Christine Evans, 2009)

As far as I know, Compton Greenfield is the only place in Gloucestershire to have this custom. It would be interesting to know how and why it crossed the Severn. Is it significant that Compton is just a couple of miles from the Gloucestershire Redwick near Pilning?

A SETTLEMENT OWING ITS ORIGIN TO THE SEVERN TUNNEL ... BUT WITH AN OLDER PAST

SUDBROOK

Sudbrook village, reached by turning off the main road by the church at Portskewett, is a village like no other in the county. It owes its origins to the construction of the Severn Tunnel between 1873 and 1876.

Among the rows of workers' cottages, the optimistically-named Sea View is of particular interest because it was constructed of concrete blocks in 1882-4, one of the earliest-known uses of concrete as a building material. Also from this period, Sudbrook's community buildings survive, including the former post office, school and the infirmary, whose long block stretches back behind the street frontage. The tunnel's contractor, Mr T.A. Walker, was a religious man, concerned that the labour force should be properly housed and provided with all necessary amenities. He is commemorated in the name of the Walker Flats in the centre of the village.

But it is the industrial monuments at the far end of the village that are Sudbrook's real claim to fame. The massive building constructed in 1886 to house six great steam-powered Cornish pumping engines dominates the view. These engines were necessary to pump out the water from the so-called Great Spring that in 1879 had flooded the workings. The massive beam engines, that raised over 10 million gallons each day, remained in place until 1962 when they were replaced by electric pumps. They would be a spectacular attraction for tourists had they survived in situ. Two engines from the smaller engine houses alongside did at least make it into preservation, one at the industrial museum in Cardiff and the other in the Science Museum, London.

Even at low tide there is a depth of nearly 60ft of water at The Shoots, a channel a quarter of a mile wide through which the river rushes. The Severn Tunnel had to be at a considerable depth below to allow its roof to be 30ft under the lowest part of the river bed. This explains its great length and the need for the pumping engines.

Alongside these buildings is the building that housed the massive fan that provided the necessary ventilation for the tunnel. Between this and the Boiler House is a tower clad in corrugated asbestos. This formed an airtight casing over a shaft 15ft in diameter. The large fan is still in place but was replaced by smaller fans underground in 1995.

The medieval chapel at Sudbrook as seen by Archdeacon Coxe.

Nearby, a path seems to be leading into a private garden but follow it to the end and you find yourself on a grassy ledge above the estuary with a magnificent view of the sweeping curve of the Second Severn Crossing. It is hard to believe it, but you are now standing in the remains of an Iron-Age hillfort! This was a strong point 4,000 years ago but was so close to the edge of the land that coastal erosion has now claimed most of the interior. The Romans recognised the fort's strategic location and it was an important stopping place on the long journey into South Wales.

Fenced off by metal railings that have seen better days are the fragmentary remains of Sudbrook's final relic – a medieval chapel, probably dating from the twelfth century. There can never have been many people living nearby. In the sixteenth century the parish was amalgamated with Portskewett and the little chapel eventually fell into disuse. Archdeacon Coxe wrote in 1801 that 'within the memory of several persons now living, divine service was performed therein. A labourer whom I met on the spot assisted forty years ago as a pallbearer and pointed out the half of a dilapidated gravestone under which the corpse was interred'.

According to local historian Richard Jones, the last burial there was an old sailor who had asked to be buried at sea. His family ignored his wishes but, says Mr Jones, 'the coastline is still eroding. He will get his way in the end!'

CHURCH-CRAWLING WEST OF THE USK
WENTLOOG

The distinctive scenery of the Caldicot Levels continues to the west of the River Usk. Maintenance of the reens, the distinctive drainage ditches that line many of the roads in this area, is the responsibility of the picturesquely-named Caldicot & Wentloog Drainage Board, an organization whose lineage goes back to the

Court of Sewers set up by Henry III. Incidentally, Somerset has the same word for the ditches but perversely spells it 'rhines', something of a trap for the unwary. According to Arthur Mee, writing in 1951, the ditches 'are up to 6ft deep and the villagers jump across them with long poles'. I am not sure whether anyone does this nowadays but it is said that you are not fully a local until you have fallen into one, but this is an honour newcomers would be wise to decline.

Although the scenery is much the same either side, for centuries the Usk was an important cultural divide. As Archdeacon Coxe put it, 'the Anglo-Normans seem to have established themselves in the Caldicot Levels at an early period. The names of the principal places and the language of the inhabitants are English.' Things were different on the western side, here he wrote 'the natives are in general Welsh and many of them scarcely understand English; consequently the churches are served in the Welsh language. In former times the population must have been considerable because these churches are large and capable of containing great congregations, though now reduced to forty or fifty persons.'

Things have changed here in the 200 years since then and the vicar of the Wentloog churches would be delighted to have fifty people in church on a Sunday. Two of the churches are still in use but the third, arguably the finest, has been sold off and is now private property and inaccessible to visitors.

Arthur Mee describes Marshfield as 'set amid peaceful by-ways', but it is quite a suburban place nowadays, just off the busy A48 between Newport and Cardiff. The church is situated down a narrow lane and in an immaculate churchyard – a contrast to the semi-derelict farm buildings (protected for some reason by CCTV cameras) opposite. Those responsible for looking after the churchyard are to be congratulated for it is a regular winner of its category in the annual 'Newport in Bloom' competition! Not that it is all so tidy that it has lost its appeal – a woodland trail round its boundary and a Wild Garden are among its attractions. Among the many interesting memorials is one made of metal, close to the two stone lions guarding the grave of Sir Henry Webb MP, a distinguished soldier, mining engineer and magistrate, who died in 1940.

St Bride's Wentloog Church has a fine tower which is a landmark across the Levels. This tower has a richly-ornamented parapet with niches containing images of the Madonna and Child, the Trinity and assorted saints. Inside the porch, to the right of the door into the church, is a stone recalling the Great Flood of 1606/7 (*see* p.58). The whole building has been affected by subsidence, having evidently settled slowly into the marshy ground, leaving the tower at a somewhat alarming angle. In 1993 the church was threatened with demolition but it was saved by conservation and stabilization work carried out over the next four years.

Another curiosity in St Brides is the Old Chapel Guest House which still has the gravestones in its garden. I assume these belong to departed chapelgoers and not folk who found cause to complain about the guest house cooking! A mile or so to the east is the low white tower of West Usk lighthouse, constructed in 1821, the first of twenty-nine lighthouses designed by James Walker for Trinity House.

Stone lions guarding the grave of Sir Henry Webb MP (died 1940), Marshfield.

The most westerly of the Wentloog villages, Peterstone is rather a sad place, buffeted by the traffic on the road towards Cardiff. Once this small village had a flourishing seaport that rivalled Cardiff but it fell into disuse long ago and nothing is left except the boundary banks of a dock. In 2000 Newman in *The Buildings of Wales* described St Peter's as 'the queen of the churches on the flat Levels beside the Severn Estuary and, indeed, the noblest and most beautiful Perpendicular church in the whole county ... the interior calm and spacious'. Since then, it has become 'Old St Peter's', almost entirely hidden behind trees and guarded by signs saying 'Private'. It is a great shame that this place of national importance is no longer open to all. 'The church is seen to best advantage by standing in the spacious chancel and looking towards the high arch of the tower,' Mee wrote. Now, that uplifting experience is denied to us.

THE LEANING TOWER OF WHITSON

WHITSON

Whitson Church stands sad and disused along a dead-end lane on the Gwent Levels, south-east of Newport. The tower leans southwards towards the Sea Wall alongside the Severn Estuary, drawn, locals said, 'by the pull of the sea'. At the top of the stair turret is the 'thimble tower', which legend says was placed there to prevent any further seaward leaning.

The lane leads on to the tiny hamlet of Great Porton but then peters out into an indistinct and often muddy footpath that leads across the fields towards Redwick.

North of the church, set back from the road that circles the Levels between Pye Corner and Goldcliff, a line of substantial farmhouses date from the time in the eighteenth century when this area was drained by a network of reens to create rich meadow and pastures.

The former church at Whitson.

A possible well head at Wilcrick.

TINY CHURCH AND THE REMAINS OF A WATER FEATURE

WILCRICK

The name Wilcrick is said to derive from the Welsh for 'bare hill' but it is the wooded slopes that now stand out prominently as seen from the M4 and A48 just west of Magor. In medieval times lepers were banished to Wilcrick Hill by fearful locals to live a safe distance away from their villages on the Levels. The old church was rebuilt in 1860 but has a medieval font and a plaque to a clergyman who was rector here for fifty-seven years in the eighteenth century.

From the churchyard, tucked away on the western side of the hill, there are pleasant views along the valley towards Pencoed Castle, with an old farmhouse prominent in the foreground. At the foot of the slope is a strange little structure like a miniature well-head, linked to carefully-constructed water channels. Quite what the purpose of this system was, I am not certain, but Wilcrick is a delightfully peaceful place to discover.

A contrast to the timelessness of Wilcrick is the futuristic modern brewery on the A48. A world away from the romantic image portrayed by the Real Ale advertisements, it comprises, in Newman's words, 'a complex of rectangular pavilions interspersed with groups of cylindrical vats … a tall steel chimneystack … [and] high-level piping.' Not an old wooden barrel or horsedrawn brewer's dray in sight!

4

Newport

HISTORIC CHURCH IN AN UNLIKELY SETTING
BETTWS

Bettws is a large 1960s housing estate two miles west of Newport. It is, of course, a considerably newer settlement than Bettws Newydd on its remote hilltop between Usk and Abergavenny. Bettws Lane links it to the city and a circular road, Monnow Way, connects the various housing areas. Bettws High School, built to cater for 1,760 children, constructed between 1969 and 1972 was described by Newman as 'a brilliant exposition of concrete construction' which 'created extraordinarily diversified spatial experiences' and was the winning design in a competition run by the Newport Education Authority in 1967. Its qualities were frankly lost on many local people, there were considerable practical problems with working in it and there was some amazement when the architectural establishment attempted, unsuccessfully, to save it from demolition in 2007. In that year inspectors from Estyn (the Welsh equivalent of Ofsted) commented that the buildings were 'no longer fit for purpose' and that their shortcomings had 'a detrimental effect on standards'. They were demolished and a new school is currently being built on the site at a cost of some £28 million.

A chilly place to be baptised – outside Bettws Church.

An unlikely survival in the district is St David's Church, a simple but heavily-restored seventeenth-century building on an older site on the southern edge of the estate. Its main claim to fame is that is was here that the Chartist leader John Frost (*see* p.81) was married in 1855 after his return from transportation to Australia. A very curious feature is an old stone font, with its lid secured by a strong chain, standing outside the west door. It must be a very chilly spot to be baptised in winter!

In 2008 the vicar, Canon Henry Davies, launched an appeal to raise £40,000 to pay for essential repairs to the church. One of its walls was reported to be sinking into the ground because of its poor foundations and there was a large crack in another.

AMPHITHEATRE WITNESSES ANCIENT TRADITION
CAERLEON

The Roman remains at Caerleon are extensive and well-preserved. The town, known as Isca Silurum, was the base for the Second Augustan Legion and the Romans' military headquarters in South Wales for over two centuries. Its position on a slight rise next to the River Usk meant that it could be defended and was free from flooding but could be easily reached by sea-going ships. Caerleon was a major settlement getting on for a millennium before there was anything of importance at Newport!

The greater part of the fortress now lies hidden beneath the modern village and the location of much else, including the barracks, is sadly unimpressive. Simon Jenkins describes how:

> ... the footings of the barracks, centurion's house and baths are sandwiched between a playing field and a housing estate.
> The bath house has been excavated, partly restored to ground level and then covered in a giant shed with viewing galleries. This is all pretty miserable ... what we are given is a twentieth-century warehouse with shopping and education paraphernalia erected on top of a heavily restored ruin.

I can see his point, although it has to be said that the visitors I saw there seemed happy enough.

It is the amphitheatre that is the real highlight. Excavated by the famous Sir Mortimer Wheeler and his wife Tessa in 1926-7 it is one of the most remarkable structures to survive from the Roman period. Possibly because of Tennyson's link with Caerleon, it was erroneously known until relatively recently as King Arthur's Round Table and believed (along with numerous other places) to have been the site of Camelot. One unusual feature is the fact that, as it was on a military base and therefore intended partly for the legion's ceremonials, the architect made provision for access to the arena from the seating area, which is not usual in Roman amphitheatres.

The Roman amphitheatre at Caerleon.

With its views towards Christchurch on the hilltop across the river, the amphitheatre is certainly a memorable location. It is often used for open-air performances of plays by Shakespeare and the like. Every May Day the locally-based Isca Morris Men dance there to greet the dawn at 6.30 a.m. This echoes the ancient pagan belief that such ceremonies bestow the sun's blessing on Mother Earth, bringing fertility and good harvests in the years to come – though I understand that these days the dancers are more motivated by the prospect of sitting down to a hearty pub breakfast afterwards!

SCHOOL FOUNDER SEEKING ATONEMENT?
CAERLEON VILLAGE SCHOOL

Caerleon is best known for its magnificent and well-preserved Roman remains but the village's school also has a fascinating tale to tell.

It was founded in the early eighteenth century under a bequest by Charles Williams, a local man who left for the Middle East under something of a cloud but made good in the end. He fled the country after killing his cousin in a duel. He ended up in Smyrna where he made his fortune and was able to return a wealthy man. He received a pardon for the killing and, when he died in 1720 at the age of eighty-seven, left a large sum of money to found a school in the town of his birth.

The original school building is still there, alongside the busy road opposite the lychgate to the churchyard. White-painted, it retains its round-headed lattice windows and a date stone reading 'Erected and Endow'd by ye Bounty of Charles Williams Esq. A Native of this Town. 1724'. It was certainly a most generous bequest and provided a building far more grandiloquent than most charity schools of the time. The differing levels of provision for the sexes, however, would certainly not find favour with modern educationists. The boys were provided with a light and lofty classroom in the centre range of the main building, reached directly from the entrance porch, but the girls had to make do with a room in the attics, lit by dormer windows!

The teaching staff were also kept well-segregated. The schoolmaster had a house in the wing to the left while the mistress was kept well away from him at the right-hand end of the building. Considerable modifications and additions to the original schoolhouse have taken place in the intervening years. It is now a primary school, so not normally open to visitors.

St Cadoc's Church, just across the road from the Williams Charity School, also benefited from Charles' will and he was later commemorated in a series of stained-glass windows dating from 1896. These tell the story of Christ's life from Annunciation to Resurrection. According to John Newman 'the style in general is Netherlandish mid-sixteenth century and great relish is taken in the vivid, if crowded, narration of the episodes.'

So, as things turned out, Charles Williams is recalled with some honour in Caerleon but whether, as the slayer of his cousin, he is held up as a good role-model in either pulpit or classroom I would not like to say!

Williams Charity School, Caerleon.

A carved head outside the Roman Museum at Caerleon.

FESTIVAL OF WOODCARVING
CAERLEON ARTS FESTIVAL

The speciality of Caerleon's annual Arts Festival in July is woodcarving. Expert sculptors from all over the country contribute to the event, using both recycled wood and standing timber in their work. A walk around the town reveals many of the pieces from past festivals displayed in appropriate locations, such as a somewhat anarchic rugby scrum at the sports ground and a Roman soldier's head outside the museum.

Other pieces go further afield, such as the three large fish standing on their tails at the Magor Marsh nature reserve.

TOMBSTONE BELIEVED TO HAVE MIRACULOUS POWERS
CHRISTCHURCH

The hilltop settlement of Christchurch, dramatically positioned with views across to the Monmouthshire hills, remains more or less aloof from the suburban sprawl east of Newport. Its church tower is a prominent landmark both from the Roman amphitheatre at Caerleon to the north and the Ringland housing estate to the south.

Alongside the church, which was sensitively restored after a disastrous fire in 1949, is the medieval Church House, a rugged building constructed from the grey local sandstone. Completing the group, which retains the feeling of a village, is the Greyhound Hotel – but this is a newcomer, dating only from about 1900. Before the modern Chepstow Road was built in the nineteenth century, the ridgeway road through Christchurch was the only route east out of Newport.

The most significant memorial in the church is a stone set into the floor of the Lady Chapel at the end of the south aisle. It bears the engraved figures of John and Isabella Colmer, who both died in 1376. Isabella wears a fetching tight-waisted gown while John's cloak is depicted thrown back to show a belted tunic worn with a dagger.

For centuries this stone was believed to have miraculous powers – but on one day only: the Eve of Ascension Day. That night parents of sick children would leave them lying on it, in the hope and expectation that they would find them cured the next morning. In 1770, it is said, sixteen children were left there. They cannot have got very much sleep!

The Colmer Stone in the Lady Chapel at Holy Trinity, Christchurch.

It would seem that the whole thing was getting a bit out of hand. The pilgrimage, if that is what it once was, had become an occasion for revelling. The inn did excellent business and it was even said that the sexton had a nasty little sideline in bribes from distraught parents. Fred Hando tells how, one Ascension Eve, in about 1810 the squire rode up to the church, demanded the key, threw out the 'pilgrims' and then rode off with the key. Perhaps he had been inspired by the story of Christ clearing the Temple in Jerusalem!

That night there was a great storm, the thunder echoing around the hills in the distance. Suddenly, without human intervention, the bells in the church tower began an unearthly peal. Two young men rode through the wild night to Llanwern to rouse the squire and bring him back to Christchurch where the bells were still ringing manically and the villagers stood terrified.

In trepidation they unlocked the church door and peered in as the flashes of lightening illuminated the darkened building. There they found 'a poor idiot boy' who had hidden when the others had been ejected from the church. Beside himself with fear at being left alone in the darkness, he had been tugging at the bell ropes to get someone to come and let him out! Hando writes that the ridicule and embarrassment of that night was enough to end the ancient tradition of the Healing Stone.

The stone may have lost its powers but the view northwards from the car park just west of church and inn is well worth the detour.

TIME CAPSULE OF THE LATE TWENTIETH CENTURY
DUFFRYN

The Duffryn Estate is part of Newport but is separated from the city by the busy A48 to the extent that it is very much a place apart.

Built by Newport Borough Council in the late 1970s, it was their last major housing estate, and – according to John Newman – with its microchip factory and government buildings Duffryn adds up to 'the most remarkable concentration of late twentieth-century architecture in the whole of Wales'.

The design of the estate is the result of a competition instituted by the Council and won by a consortium committed to the theories of planning devised in the 1960s by the architecture department at Cambridge University. Its characteristic feature is the ingeniously-located wriggling terraces of two-storey dwellings that continue round the entire perimeter of the 96-acre site. Footpaths interrupt these terraces to lead through to back gardens and the open ground beyond. To quote Newman again: 'These terraces come forwards and recede to form irregular octagonal courtyards built-up on seven of their eight sides'. With 977 housing units in the area, Duffryn is a low-density development and at its heart is an area of woodland and open space which takes up almost half the estate.

Above left: Housing units, Duffryn Estate.

Above right: Inmos microchip factory, Duffryn.

So far, so good, perhaps but the house fronts are drab and uniform in the extreme – Stalinist-looking slabs faced in reddish-brown to mushroom brick with cream-coloured asbestos cement above, topped off with sombre brown tile-hanging. As Newman observes, 'the District Amenities Centre, planned for the south-west corner, was unfortunately never built so one of the principal planning aims at Duffryn, to create a largely self-sufficient development, was not achieved'. There are, however, schools and a pub, which looks like a broken-off fragment of one of the housing units.

Newman describes the Inmos microchip factory as 'an unforgettable image as well as a structure as logical as it is flamboyant'. It was built by Richard Rogers & Partners in 1982 – Rogers' keenness for the essential services to be on the outside of the building, coupled with the need for a sterile environment inside, combined to create a stunning futuristic design. Together with the Central Statistical Office (1973) and the Patent Office (1990), the factory completes a memorable group of buildings.

Wandering round this area might be difficult but Duffryn is a time capsule of the late twentieth century and well worth seeing.

JOHN FROST AND THE CHARTISTS
JOHN FROST SQUARE, NEWPORT

John Frost Square is a rather bleak and windswept place. Part of a bland 1970s redevelopment in the centre of Newport, it was for several years dominated by a massive hoarding proclaiming the benefits of the stylish new Friars Walk shopping complex 'Opening 2010' but abandoned the year before, a victim of the recession. Some years before, it had lost the one thing that had made it at all distinctive – the massive Automaton Clock designed as Newport's contribution to the 1992 Ebbw Vale Garden Festival and brought back here after the festival ended.

Yet the square's name recalls a time when Newport was at the centre of events that ultimately had a significant influence on Britain's political evolution – the Chartist Uprising of 1839. Approaching the square from the direction of Upper Dock Street and the market, shoppers pass through a cavernous subway. All along one wall, almost impossible to see in the gloom, is a tile mosaic by Kenneth Budd which tells the story of this ill-starred enterprise.

Chartism was a movement that found support among the underprivileged. Its radical programme for social reform called for all men over twenty-one to have the vote; secret ballots; abolition of the requirement for MPs to own property of a certain value; MPs to be paid (so that working-class men could afford to stand for Parliament); and parliamentary constituencies to be of equal size; and annual elections. All but the last eventually came to pass but at the time the Chartists were viewed with fear and suspicion by the authorities – and not without good reason, perhaps.

The movement's leaders were a mixed bunch with different ideas about how to achieve their objectives. Some thought change could be achieved by peaceful persuasion but others, including John Frost, believed that more violent methods would be necessary. They found their support amid the downtrodden industrial workers of industrial South Wales which became a hotbed of enthusiasm for the cause.

In November 1839 the movement's leaders in Monmouthshire, including John Frost, came to believe that if their supporters marched *en masse* into Newport and took control of the town, they could trigger an insurrection nationally and achieve their aims. They were fatally over-optimistic.

When they arrived, they found that the mayor had summoned a detachment of soldiers from the barracks. The armed men had taken up position in the Westgate Hotel, strategically situated in the heart of Newport. What happened next is disputed but within minutes the soldiers had opened fire, killing over twenty people.

The events of 4 November 1839 have acquired long-lasting significance in Newport. Like other similar occasions since, all over the world, they have generated their own mythology of massacre and martyrdom. Each year the anniversary is solemnly commemorated. Children do school projects about Chartism. There is a memorial, in the form of three somewhat ambiguous sculptures by Christopher Kelly, outside the Westgate Hotel and a stone plaque to the victims by the main door of the cathedral. It is said that the holes from the musket balls can still be seen in the pillars of the hotel entrance (or would be if it had not been blocked to discourage vagrants from congregating there). Sceptics, however, point out that these holes were exactly were they would be needed for fixing metal gates to the pillars. The building – no longer a hotel, incidentally – dates from 1886 so is clearly not the one that witnessed this tragic event.

Whether the protestors were brave defenders of justice or a mere unruly mob, whipped up by professional agitators, causes debate in the columns of the *Argus* every year.

Above and top: Chartist memorial mosaic by Kenneth Budd.

Right: The entrance to the former Westgate Hotel, Newport.

BRITAIN'S FIRST PUBLIC CEMETERY
ST WOOLOS, NEWPORT

St Woolos Cemetery, with its ornate Victorian funeral monuments, is an atmospheric place – so atmospheric in fact that it was used as a setting for the 2008 *Doctor Who* Christmas Special. David Tennant and Catherine Tate were chased around the gravestones by the evil Cybermen who loomed out of the synthetic mist in a suitably terrifying manner.

Confusingly, St Woolos Cemetery is not right next to the cathedral of the same name but a mile or so west of it along Bassaleg Road. In between is St Woolos Hospital, which I suppose could be poignantly apt.

The cemetery is very extensive – it must be one of the largest municipal graveyards in the country – neatly kept but not over-manicured. When it opened in 1850 it was, in fact, the first public cemetery in Britain. The south-eastern corner with its two chapels is particularly rich in weeping angels, urns and florid tributes to Newport's merchants and Master Mariners.

Less exalted folk are remembered here as well. A rough-hewn obelisk commemorates thirty-nine dock construction workers who died in July 1909, drowned in glutinous mud and seawater when the sides of their excavation collapsed without warning (*see* p.85). The memorial carries a poem and a dedication to those who lost their lives. It was paid for by their employers, the Scottish engineering firm, Easton, Gibb & Son.

By the Risca Road entrance to the cemetery is a memorial bearing another tragic story but it also bears witness to a belief in an afterlife that was more common a century ago than now. It is in the form of a massive stone lighthouse, symbolic of 'Jesus Christ – The Light of the World' and was erected 'In Loving Memory of

Memorials in St Woolos Cemetery.

Winnie, beloved adopted daughter of Edwin and Annie Parsons, who Fell Asleep in Jesus, 3rd July 1907, aged 27.' Edwin and Annie lived on without her, dying in their sixties two years apart in the early 1920s.

At the foot of the lighthouse is carved 'No other foundation than Jesus'.

But faiths other than the Christian one have their place in St Woolos Cemetery, both Jewish and Islamic. In *Real Newport* (2006), Ann Drysdale describes her attempts to find the Jewish graves in the adjacent Coed-Melyn Park:

> There's an old cemetery by the gate, but it has been closed for a long time now. There's a newer plot further into the park … At the far end of the park I found a small crowded burial ground. Through the wire fence I could make out Hebrew inscriptions on the stones – but there was no obvious way in … When I finally found the gate it was padlocked. It was not difficult to see why. Vandals had sprayed graffiti and overturned headstones. Everything inside had been sullied and spoiled.

There is nothing more to be said.

BOY HERO OF 1909
TOM TOYA LEWIS

With the Transporter Bridge visible in the distance, Commercial Street in Newport leads southwards from the city centre towards Pill and the docks. On the right, just before you pass St John's Church, is a pub with a curious name – The Tom Toya Lewis. Visitors to Newport might wonder who he was.

Tom Lewis was a lad of seventeen when he found unexpected fame as the hero of the Newport Docks disaster of 2 July 1909. He was an unlikely candidate for heroism – a gambler on both cards and horses, he had already come to the attention of the police. Yet on that awful summer's day he showed a level of bravery that was totally unexpected.

Just before the siren sounded to mark the end of the working day the sides of a new lock being built to link the dock to the open water collapsed without warning, trapping the men working below. Some were able to scramble to safety but many others were buried by hundreds of tons of earth and mud. It is believed that the cause of the tragedy was saturation of the earth from the bed of the river, combined with the effects of a particularly wet summer.

As those who were able cried for help, young Tom climbed down into the collapsed workings to rescue a man called Bardill whose arm was trapped by a 12-inch beam. He scrabbled at the wet earth in a vain attempt to free his fellow worker's arm but eventually, as a further collapse seemed imminent, he was ordered to return to safety.

The Tom Toya Lewis,
Commercial Street, Newport.

'Faced with leaving the man he was trying to save he began to cry tears of frustration,' Tom's grandson (also called Tom Lewis) told *Argus* journalist Mike Buckingham on the 100th anniversary of the accident. 'Ever afterwards, if anyone mentioned the docks disaster, he would fill up.'

Thanks to Tom's heroic efforts, Bardill was in fact rescued without serious injury but at least thirty-nine of his fellow workers lost their lives. The exact number of casualties will never be known because, unbelievably, no attempt was made at the time to check on the whereabouts of the casual labourers employed. Those bodies recovered were buried in a mass grave at St Woolos Cemetery but, according to Mr Buckingham, 'up to sixteen men lie for ever entombed by the River Usk's mud and gravel'.

Tom Toya Lewis was acclaimed as the hero of the hour and shortly afterwards he was summoned to London to receive the Albert Medal 'for conspicuous bravery' from King Edward VII. There had also to be a villain, and the scapegoat was an unfortunate site supervisor named Ratcliffe who – somewhat conveniently – had subsequently died from the injuries that he received. None of the directors of the construction company was ever brought to trial for negligence.

'Well done, Tom Lewis,' King Edward had said as he pinned the medal on his chest. 'I shall expect to hear more of you.' But Tom, who had only a few weeks before been convicted of stealing lead, was to make several more appearances before the local magistrates – which was probably not what the king had in mind!

Even his grandson admits that his grandfather had been 'a bit of a rogue'. In an article to mark the anniversary, Mr Buckingham writes that 'documents which passed between civil servants suggested that a seventeen-year-old boy, written off as a tearaway but who went on to display great bravery, could be used as a good example for other erring youths – an early attempt at positive spin'.

At 5 p.m. on 2 July 2009 Tom's grandson threw a memorial wreath into Newport Docks. It was a sombre and fitting tribute. Another tribute came in the form of a choral work, *A Newport Elegy* by Michael Elliot, a former County Librarian who studied music under composer Lennox Berkeley in the 1940s. 'It's a bit discordant at times, to reflect the awfulness of what happened,' Mr Elliot told the *Argus*.

Tom Toya Lewis, who died in the late 1960s, is not the only Newport hero to have a pub named after him. Close to the station is one named after John Linton, Newport's VC. (*see* p.89)

CITY CENTRE SCULPTURES
NEWPORT

A feature of Newport City Centre has been the provision of modern sculpture to enliven and add interest to streets and public open spaces.

One of the most striking is Sebastian Boyesen's life-size bronze bull, dated 1995. It relates to the medieval legend of the vision of St Gwynllyw which indicated where the chapel, which was the original nucleus of St Woolos Cathedral should be constructed. This is somewhat incongruously located in the bleak shopping development north of John Frost Square. Another Boyesen figure is outside the market building in Upper Dock Street. Described by John Newman as 'temptingly-pattable', it is of 'the little piggy that went to market, a basket of fruit and vegetables strapped to its back'. The market building, designed in 1887 in the manner of a Flemish cloth hall, is 'the most conspicuous sign of Newport's late Victorian civic pride'.

Outside the former Westgate Hotel in Commercial Street a complex group of bronzes by Christopher Kelly (1989) commemorates the building's importance in the history of Chartism. Three groups of figures (The Ideal City, Still Life and Apotheosis) are intended to represent the Chartist ideals of Unity, Prudence and Energy. The symbolism is somewhat obscure – Newman observes that 'it says something for the confidence of the Borough Council, which commissioned the sculpture, in both the piety and the intelligence of the people of Newport that they have placed such an elliptical work at the heart of the town'.

Further down Commercial Street the Newport-born poet W.H. Davies, author of *Autobiography of a Super-Tramp* and the memorable couplet 'What is this life if full of care, We have no time to stand and stare?', is commemorated by a strange bronze by Paul Bothwell Kincaid (1990). This is described as 'a standing, shrouded figure, apparently with hands on hips, set between a pair of branches on which doves perch'.

Bronze Bull by Sebastian Boyesen (1995).

At the bottom of Commercial Street, where it meets Kingsway and George Street, is the romantically-named Mariners' Green. It does not quite live up to its name, but here, on an island in the busy road, is the Merchant Navy Memorial of 1991. Also by Boyesen, it depicts a seated figure of Navigation.

'THE WAVE' AND A NAVAL HERO
NEWPORT

At the western end of the Town Bridge, across the road from the sad fragmentary remains of the castle, stands 'The Wave', a striking piece of modern metal artwork, massively controversial when it was put up in 1990, but now becoming as much of a symbol of Newport as the iconic Transporter Bridge.

The work of Peter Fink, it is described by John Newman as 'two scarlet vaulting braces converging to suspend a scarlet hoop, from which hangs a triangle of triangles, each painted in a primary colour. Its significance, as a tribute to Newport's steelmakers and seafarers is easily understood, and it can as readily be enjoyed as a lithe virile form'.

I am not sure that I can share Mr Newman's confidence in its clarity of meaning. Ann Drysdale clearly is not impressed. In *Real Newport* (2006) she observes that:

… there isn't much to it really. If you see it from a train coming over the bridge, it looks like an M-for McDonald's, while from the other side of the river it looks like a comatose comma. The only human endeavour left for it to celebrate is the evidence of intrepid climbing by untalented graffiti artists to see who can leave the highest tag. The annotations are of the usual sort. Representations of unfeasible genitalia and dates of when assorted saddos 'woz ya'.

Such characters would have seemed an alien species to the man commemorated by a much smaller unobtrusive monument in its shadow. A simple locally-made black bollard is inscribed in memory of 'Commander J.W. Linton, V.C., D.S.C., R.N. 1905-1943. Lost with all hands aboard H.M. Submarine 'Turbulent' in the Mediterranean, 1943'.

John Wallace 'Tubby' Linton is Newport's only recipient of the Victoria Cross. According to the official citation in the *London Gazette*, the *Turbulent*, under Linton's command, was responsible for sinking nearly 100,000 tons of enemy shipping, including a cruiser, destroyer, U-boat and twenty-eight supply ships. The *Turbulent* went missing without any warning or 'Mayday' message and is believed to have been sunk in a minefield.

Every year a dignified memorial service takes place on the Town Bridge. Newport's civic leaders come together to remember the town's wartime hero and a wreath is cast onto the cloudy waters of the Usk as it nears the sea.

Above left: The Wave (with the remains of Newport Castle in the background).

Above right: The John Wallace Linton, Newport. Soon after this photograph was taken the sign was removed and eventually replaced with one merely giving the name of the pub.

CULT TV CONNECTIONS

BELLE VUE PARK, NEWPORT

Newport Council is justly proud of its municipal parks which are well-maintained and much-appreciated by local people. In the crowded suburbs to the east of the city centre Beechwood Park is a welcome area of beauty. Beechwood House, an elegant Victorian building, has recently been adapted for use by small business ventures. Belle Vue Park to the west of the centre, close to St Woolos' Cathedral, has everything a city park should have: bandstand, tea room, tennis courts, ornamental trees, smooth lawns and colourful flower beds. Unfortunately, both parks suffer problems with youngsters indulging in underage drinking, vandalism and general antisocial behaviour, especially on summer evenings.

'Druid Circle',
Belle Vue Park,
Newport.

Twenty-first-century youth would undoubtedly be a source of pain to Lord Tredegar who gave the land for the park in 1891. A national competition was held for its design which was won by one Thomas Mawson. His proposed layout was commended and contracts signed when it was discovered that he had misread the map which he had been given and designed it all for a neighbouring plot of land which is now the site of the Royal Gwent Hospital. It must have been an embarrassing moment for all concerned! However, the young Mawson clearly had talent and he went on to do successful designs for Holker Hall and Rydal Hall in the Lake District and the Duffryn Botanic Gardens in Cardiff.

Belle Vue Park's most recent claim to fame is that, like St Woolos' Cemetery (*see* p.84), it has been used for the filming of an episode of *Doctor Who*, starring David Tennant and Billie Piper and, in this case, the dog K9. Ann Drysdale comments in *Real Newport* that she observed that the creature was not on a lead, in direct contravention of council byelaws!

There is a less well-known link to another cult TV programme of much longer ago. In the 1960s the success of *The Man from UNCLE* resulted in a series of paperback novels based on the characters. One of these, *The Stone Cold Dead in the Market Affair* by John Oram, was (somewhat improbably) set partly in Newport. My wife is a dedicated *UNCLE* fan and recently I found myself walking around the city with her looking for places mentioned in the book! Our discoveries later featured in an article in *The Network*, the UNCLE fan club magazine.

The story begins in a pub in Market Street. Illya Kuryakin, the character played in the series by David McCallum, then goes by bus from outside the Market Hall up to Stow Hill and walks down to Belle Vue Park. Mr Oram obviously knew Newport well because, even forty years later, almost all the landmarks he mentions can still be seen. His descriptions of the houses in Stow Park Avenue and the features of the park are completely accurate, including the Gorsedd Stone Circle under the oak trees. This was erected in 1896 for the Eisteddfod held the following year and can still be found more than a century later.

Like the devotees of *Star Trek* and *Doctor Who*, *UNCLE* fans, with their esoteric conversations and catchphrases, are a dedicated bunch. Perhaps Newport Corporation should take advantage of this unlikely source of interest and promote an 'Illya Kuryakin Trail' around Belle Vue Park!

THE SOMERTON TARDIS

CHEPSTOW ROAD, NEWPORT

A landmark on Newport's Chepstow Road for many years has been the Somerton Tardis – a blue police phone box of the type that no longer exists but which was immortalised by the *Doctor Who* series.

The Somertan Tardis.

At some time in the past someone painted a long multi-coloured scarf, as worn by the Doctor in his Tom Baker incarnation, on the side facing the main road. The colours are faded now and the box has seen better days. Even so, it was a shock when it was recently threatened with demolition. Local residents rallied to its support and their campaign featured in the *South Wales Argus* and on BBC Wales news programmes.

The box stands at the junction with Somerton Crescent and Hawthorn Avenue. When I photographed it in September 2009 it was fenced off and looking somewhat sorry for itself. Perhaps Doctor Who himself, with the assistance of one of his glamorous young female companions, will transport it back to its heyday!

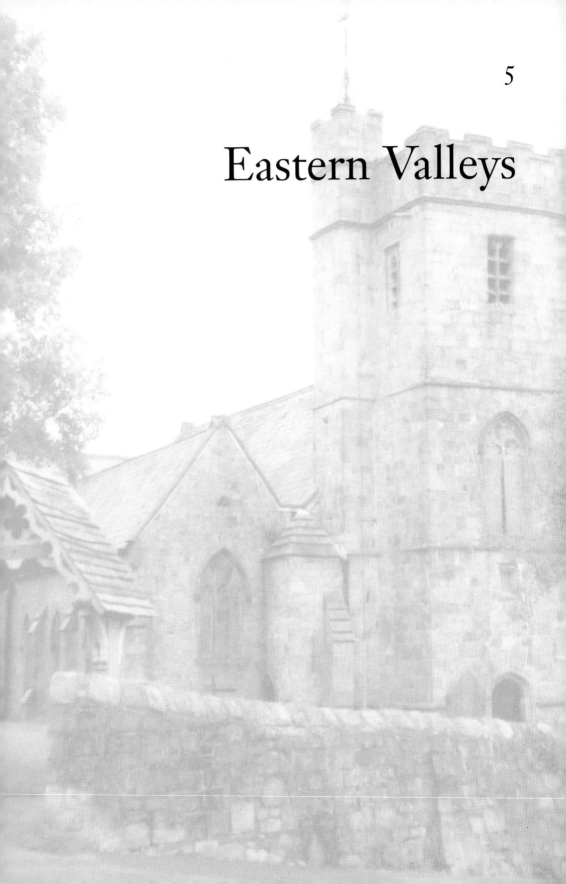

5

Eastern Valleys

ARTWORK ADDS 'INTEREST'
TO MODERN SHOPPING CENTRE

CWMBRAN

Overlooking Gwent Square, at the heart of the shopping area, are a series of mural panels designed by Henry and Joyce Collins and unveiled by Sir William Crawshay, chairman of the Welsh Arts Council, in 1974. Presented to the New Town by the Cwmbran Arts Trust, they feature imaginative scenes from the area's history. The first portrays Caradog, the leader of the Silures, who were defeated by the Romans in AD 51. Taken to Rome, where he was led through the streets in chains, his dignified bearing so impressed Emperor Claudius that Caradog (also known to history as Caractacus) was given his liberty.

Other panels depict the Romans at Caerleon, the Norman Conquest, Welsh bowmen at the Battle of Crecy and a medieval monk of Llantarnam Abbey. The series is completed by depictions of mining and steelworking – themselves now part of Monmouthshire's past. The history of Cwmbran New Town itself is honoured in a tiled panel put up nearby to marks its first fifty years, 1949 to 1999.

Above left: One of two sculptures at Llantarnam Grange, Cwmbran – I cannot be sure whether this one is 'the family group' or 'the footballers'.

Above right: The Cwmbran Giant.

In the Water Garden, a sunken area on the edge of the shopping centre, can be found six tiled panels which were on the wall of the now-demolished Up and Under public house. There is also a bronze sculpture of an otter by Adrian Sorrell, dedicated to the memory of Tessa Hodge, formerly chairman of the Arts Trust. The 'Cwmbran Giant' by Peter Nicholas depicts a giant carrying a young child out of the water and towards the town centre. I hope it does not give any toddlers nightmares! Describing it as 'a Millennium statement,' the artist wrote that 'the head of the child is impressed into the main figure like a coin. They are indivisible.'

Unfortunately, the Water Garden was looking rather neglected when I visited, the rectangular concrete pond drained for a programme of maintenance that seemed to be going on for a long time.

Close to the Centre is Llantarnam Grange Arts Centre, home to two sculptures, strikingly modern in their day but over forty years old now: 'The Family Group', the work of David Horn in 1965 and 'The Footballers' (by Helega Prosser, 1966). 'Kate's Bears' by Anthony Stevens, a Welsh Arts Council commission in 1973, are at the Ysgol Gymraeg.

In 2001 Torfaen Council commissioned a series of sculpted wooden seats from Pembrokeshire-based sculptor Robert Jakes. These can be found near the old canal at various locations, including Garndiffaith, Griffithstown Railway Museum and Forge Row. Pupils from Fairwater High School were involved in decorating these seats with images made with copper and galvanised nails.

Prominent close to the town centre is a slim twenty-two-storey tower block designed by Gordon Redfern. He conceived it as 'a campanile or cathedral spire to serve as a landmark for travellers'.

INDUSTRIAL HISTORY IN A RURAL SETTING
GOYTRE WHARF

I came to Goytre Wharf the hard way – plodding up the Monmouthshire & Brecon Canal towpath all the way from Pontypool. It was not a nice day. The weather forecast had promised fine weather with the possibility of a few showers. It seemed more like the other way about. The rain started as I walked across Pontypool Park on my way to join the towpath and continued until I was passing near Mamhilad! A boat was parked on a trailer at Ty-poeth Farm, up the hillside to the left of the canal a mile or so out of town. It looked ready for action. Did they know something I didn't, I wondered?

Despite the rain and the slippery path, it was a delightful walk with lovely views across the countryside. Goytre Wharf, when I eventually got there about two hours later, was a fascinating place. Newman calls it 'one of the most complete and eloquent expressions of the impact on late eighteenth-century agriculture of the new developments in industry and transport'.

Figures at
Goytre Warf.

You reach the site from the canal towpath by walking down a short steep path and then turning right under the arch of the aqueduct. When you emerge from this arch the most prominent features are the three limekilns, looking like low railway arches, and the diminutive stone cottage built for the operator of the weighbridge. Standing out ahead of you, at a higher level, is what was the home of the manager of the whole enterprise. Painted white, it is now the visitors' centre, café and shop.

By the kilns are two lifelike figures of men hard at work. There is a short length of tramway track and an old truck. The whole complex has been excellently restored by British Waterways. One imaginative feature is a glass screen through which you can view the site. The outlines of the surviving buildings as they once were are drawn onto the glass, together with other features of the place in its heyday. There is also a thriving canal-boat hire business.

You do not have to travel to Goytre Wharf by boat or on foot, although these would be the best if you want to get the most authentic experience. It is also accessible by road (signposted off the A4042 between Pontypool and Abergavenny).

RECALLING A CATHOLIC MARTYR

LLANTARNAM ABBEY

The Old Post Office (now a private house) in Newport Road, Llantarnam, part of Cwmbran, was long ago the site of a smithy, the scene of the arrest of a Catholic priest, Father David Lewis, at the time of the public hysteria whipped up by Titus Oates in the reign of Charles II. Catholics were viewed with grave suspicion and under pressure to conform to the teachings of the Established Church. Oates and his confederate Israel Tongue put before Parliament fabricated evidence of a so-called 'Popish Plot' to assassinate the King and replace him with his Catholic brother, James.

Lewis had been born at Abergavenny in 1616 and raised as a Protestant but at the age of sixteen he converted to Catholicism while living in Paris. He was ordained priest there in 1642 and became a Jesuit five years later. He returned to South Wales and was one of a number of priests based at Cwm near Monmouth and supported by Edward Morgan, the Catholic owner of Llantarnam Abbey, which his family had acquired after the Dissolution of the Monasteries. Lewis was the nephew of Morgan's wife, Lady Frances. One of the other places where he celebrated Mass was Gunter House in Abergavenny (*see* p.25).

With anti-Catholic feeling at its height, Lewis was betrayed; it is said, by a servant girl at the Abbey. He was taken back to Abergavenny in some sort of triumphal procession, like a Prisoner of War being marched through the streets facing the catcalls of the populace. It was alleged that he had styled himself 'Bishop of Llandaff' but this was later revealed to be one of Titus Oates' lies. No evidence of any link to a Popish Plot could be found but he was convicted of breaking a statute from Elizabeth I's time which made it high treason to be ordained abroad as a Catholic priest and then return to England and say Mass. Found guilty, he was taken to London to be interrogated by Oates and then brought back to Monmouthshire for the death sentence to be carried out.

The Old Post Office, Llantarnam.

The execution took place at Usk in August 1679. It was a shambles. The official executioner and his assistants had refused to carry it out. A convicted felon agreed to do the deed, in return for a free pardon, but he too fled. The hanging, drawing and quartering was eventually performed by a local blacksmith but it is said that afterwards no local people would give him any work, such was the esteem in which Father Lewis was held. Ironically, it was not long before Oates himself was discredited. In May 1680 he was tried for perjury and condemned to be 'whipped, degraded and pilloried'. Judge Jefferies (no pure innocent himself as it turned out) said of him, 'He has deserved punishment more than the laws of the land can inflict.' His grave is in the churchyard at Usk (see p.50).

Father David Lewis was Beatified by the Roman Catholic Church in 1929 and Canonized by Pope Paul VI in 1970 as one of the 'Forty Martyrs of England and Wales'. His portrait can be seen in the chapel corridor at Llantarnam Abbey and a Blue Plaque marks the site of his arrest.

RORKE'S DRIFT HERO STILL REMEMBERED
LLANTARNAM

Although now administered as part of Cwmbran, Llantarnam retains a recognisably old village centre around the fifteenth-century church and the Greenhouse Inn.

Close to the entrance to the churchyard is the grave of John Fielding who (as the wording on the headstone has it) 'as Private John Williams won the Victoria Cross at the Battle of Rorke's Drift during the Zulu War in January 1879'.

Rorke's Drift was a British outpost guarding the crossing point of the Buffalo River on the road to Natal. It was a mission station being used as a field hospital. Following the Zulu victory at Isandhlwana, it was held, against overwhelming odds, by just eighty British soldiers.

A force of 4,000 Zulus was bearing down on the hospital's two buildings which stood about thirty yards apart. Barricades were hastily thrown up between them, using whatever materials came to hand. Williams and two other soldiers found themselves at one end of the station with no direct access to their wounded colleagues, as the doors into the hospital section were at the far end of the building.

Gradually, as the overwhelming force of attackers moved forward, Williams and his colleagues hacked their way back towards the wards, Williams wielding a pickaxe to break down the intervening walls and dragging his fellow defenders (who were now injured) back with him.

The Zulu attack had begun in the afternoon and it lasted until dawn. Six times they broke through the defences but were pushed back. The roof of the building was set ablaze but eventually the heroic band of defenders got the upper hand and the Zulus were repulsed. It was a turning point in the war and Private Williams was feted as a national hero. He was one of eight men awarded the VC for their work that day.

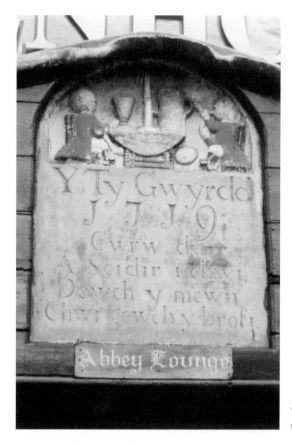

The date stone above the entrance to the Greenhouse Inn, Llantarnam.

It is not clear why John Fielding served in the British Army under a different name but it is as Fielding not Williams that he is commemorated. He survived the war and returned to Llantarnam, living until 1932 when – in a world that had changed beyond recognition in the intervening half century – he died at the age of seventy-five. His gravestone was erected in Llantarnam churchyard by his old regiment, the 2nd Btn, 24th Rgt. of Foot, South Wales Borderers, bearing the postscript 'Lest We Forget'.

John Fielding certainly has not been forgotten at Llantarnam and his heroism is acknowledged every year at his graveside. On 26 January 2008 those taking part then processed across the road to a new housing development named John Fielding Gardens. Here, in the presence of civic dignitaries, members of the Comrades Association of the South Wales Borderers and the Rt Hon. Paul Murphy, Secretary of State for Wales and MP for Torfaen, a new memorial was dedicated. It is a block of slate carved by Teucer Wilson to represent '*y coru hirlas*', a horn of plenty, used by the Welsh in antiquity as a drinking vessel or blown to sound the alarm if danger threatened. Part of its inscription reads 'Bear thou the rich foaming mead to the brave, the dragons of battle, the sons of the free'.

I am not sure whether 'rich foaming mead' is on offer at the Greenhouse Inn, but above the door of this building is an ornamental datestone reading 'Y Ty Gwyrdd 1719'. It shows two red-coated gentlemen sitting at a table which bears a candle, large flagon and a beaker. The verse underneath, '*Cwrw da/ A Soidir i chwi/ Dewch y mewn/ Chwi gewch y brofi*', invites the traveller to step inside and taste good ale and cider. Perhaps they should now toast the memory of Llantarnam's nineteenth-century hero!

HISTORIC BUILDINGS DIVIDED IN BOUNDARY DISPUTE
LLANYRAFON

Not much more than the width of Llanfrechfa Road separates Llanyrafon Mill from the Manor Farm, a mile or so from the centre of Cwmbran – but it makes a huge difference to their prospects of funding.

Manor Farm recently received a £1.3 million grant to restore the building but the Friends of Llanyrafon Mill complain that they can only hope for tiny community council grants for their project. A quirk of local authority boundaries is responsible for this curious state of affairs: the farmhouse is in the rural Llanyrafon South ward, making it eligible for rural regeneration funding, while the mill is in Llanyrafon North which is classified as urban, so these grants are not available.

The Friends are a voluntary group working to turn their building back into a working mill. There is documentary evidence that there was a mill here in 1632, but it probably predates that. It was latterly a three-storey corn mill with an overshot wheel. It served a large area, extending as far as Tredegar House at Newport.

Above left: Llanyrafon Mill.

Above right: Llanyrafon Manor Farm.

Water to drive the mill was taken from the Afon Llwyd about half a mile north of the site and was returned to the river below Manor Farm. Production of flour eventually ceased in 1951 and the building became derelict. Severe damage was caused by a fire in 1971.

Torfaen Council became involved and reroofed the mill in the 1980s to protect the machinery inside. The Friends were formed in 1995 and now open the mill to the public on summer weekends, Bank Holidays and at other times by arrangement. In 2006 the Heritage Lottery Fund confirmed that they would support the restoration project but up to now no bid has been mounted because Torfaen was unable to find the necessary match funding, partly because the North ward was seen as an affluent area.

By contrast, preliminary restoration work has already begun on Manor Farm and it is scheduled to open to the public in 2012. When I visited, the house was hidden behind high walls and dense foliage so little of it could be seen. It has an impressive three-storeyed entrance porch, evidence that it was once more than a mere farmhouse. It dates from the late sixteenth century and retains many of its original features. However, its eighteenth-century staircase was moved across the road to what is now the Commodore Hotel in the 1890s.

DEATHS OF THREE AIRMAN AND A CLERGYMAN AGED 102

MAMHILAD

Mamhilad, three miles from Pontypool, may be best known to some for its Industrial Estate alongside the A4042. The modernist-style Dupont Factory (formerly British Nylon Spinners) was built in 1947-8. It is quite a landmark because of its massive rectangular 'spinning tower'.

A mile or so north, off the main road, is the tiny village. Visitors enter the churchyard over a stile formed from the gravestone of one Aaron Morris, who died in 1680. What he would have thought of this indignity we shall never know.

The glory of the church is its well-preserved west gallery. Here the rustic 'village band' of musicians would accompany the hymns and chants in the days before they were replaced with harmoniums and organs in Victorian times. Many churches once had galleries of this type but they are now comparatively rare.

Often, as at Mamhilad, these galleries incorporated timbers that originally came from the medieval rood-loft, taken down at the Reformation. Here visitors can see the bressumer, the big horizontal beam that supported the wall above, and pierced traceried panels which display the skills of the carpenters.

On the south wall of the chancel is a memorial to Revd Christopher Cook who died in 1927 after serving as rector here from 1855 to 1925! He died at the age of 102 after a fall while out walking in icy conditions.

The west gallery (which was originally part of a medieval rood loft) at St Illtyd's Church, Mamhilad.

It is a delightful little church, but unfortunately it seems to be locked most of the time. If you do get the chance to see the interior, it is well worth the effort. A steep lane opposite the church leads up to a lofty bridge over the Monmouthshire & Brecon Canal. From here you can walk either to Pontypool or Goytre Wharf.

High above Mamhilad, near the summit of Mynydd Garn-wen a couple of miles north-west, is a memorial to the young crew of an RAF Bristol Blenheim bomber which crashed onto the mountain, returning to their base in Hampshire after a training flight in September 1940. Weather conditions and visibility were very poor at the time and the pilot, like his two colleagues aged only twenty, would have been relying on his instruments. A memorial stone was put up in 2000 on the sixtieth anniversary of this tragedy which is now marked by a simple service on Remembrance Day.

'THE GLORY BE TO THEE O GOD ALONE'
PONTNEWYDD

One of the best websites that I discovered while researching for this book was that created by Nigel Jones, who somehow also finds the time to serve as a local councillor in Cwmbran. The site, www.cwmbran.info, covers the history and facilities of the New Town, including outlying districts such as Llantarnam and Pontnewydd, as well as personal reminiscences of local people.

I was particularly taken with an item contributed by a Mr Stan Edwards of Pontnewydd. It illustrates the strong Christian faith that is still a feature of life in South Wales, perhaps more than in some other parts of Britain. Readers will, I hope, understand why I have not been able to include a photograph of the memorial described and why it is probably better that this is the case. It is simply too personal.

'The Glory be to Thee, O God Alone'. The memorial is somewhere on the hillside overlooking Potnewydd.

Mr Edwards describes how, sometime in the mid 1950s, he was climbing up the steep hill that overlooks Pontnewydd. He came upon a rock upon which someone had carved the text 'The Glory be to thee, O God Alone'. 'Until recently,' he writes, 'no one I had spoken to knew of its existence. The person who carved it obviously wanted to carve something with humility so personal that no one could congratulate him on his workmanship. He/she must have valued this secret place and understood the meaning of God alone getting all the Glory.'

He describes how, in his younger days, he took his boys up to see it and vowed then that one day he would return to 'that very steep dingle' while still able to do so. He is now in his sixties and on a Bank Holiday in the summer of 2007 he climbed up to search for the stone once more. 'It was hard to find it and I am not as fit as I was,' he acknowledged.

But he got there and I am glad that he did.

THE ART OF JAPANNING
CRANE STREET STATION, PONTYPOOL

Impressive murals at the site of Pontypool's former Crane Street station recall the art of Japanning that once made the town famous all over the world.

In 1660 Thomas Allgood moved from Northampton to take up a post at the ironworks belonging to John Hanbury, a family still famous in the industrial history of South Wales. Here he experimented with extracting oils from coal and was able to produce a varnish with properties equalled to that used on the lacquered goods from Japan that were all the rage at the time.

He set up a factory to produce similar products in Pontypool but the commercial development needed was left to his sons Edward and John, who

Japanning mural, Crane Street, Pontypool.

made the technical improvements necessary for the factory to be commercially successful. This apparently involved industrial espionage in the unlikely setting of Bedfordshire. Archdeacon Coxe wrote enigmatically that 'for the purpose of discovering the secret Edward repaired to Woburn in the character of a beggar and, acting the part of a buffoon, gradually obtained access to the workshops and was permitted to inspect the various processes.' The process involved thin sheets of iron or tinplate being cleaned in a bath of acid and then lacquered and polished several times. Examples of Japan ware can be seen in the town's museum.

In 1761, however, there seems to have been a family row. While John remained in Pontypool, his younger brother decamped to Usk where he set up a rival establishment. Fashions changed and by 1800 the demand for Japan ware had greatly diminished. The Pontypool factory closed in 1822, though Usk lasted until 1860.

Pontypool around 1800 had been a curious mixture of industrial and agricultural. Archdeacon Coxe wrote that it was:

... a straggling place containing 250 houses and 1,500 souls. Several neat habitations and numerous shops present the appearance of thriving prosperity, notwithstanding the dusky aspect of the town occasioned by the adjacent forges ... The district is the principal mart for the natives of the mountainous district and the weekly market is the cheapest in Monmouthshire.

Coxe, as an educated Englishman, was patronising in the extreme about the upland Welsh, whom he described curiously as 'mountaineers':

It was a pleasing amusement to mix in these crowded meetings to observe the frank and simple manner of the hardy mountaineers and endeavour, in asking the price of their provisions, to extract a Saxon word from this British progeny.

There is still a market in Pontypool, where I was startled, among other things, to see on sale packets of decorative stickers for wheelie-bins, a triumph of Western civilisation that had previously escaped me – but whether it is still the cheapest in Monmouthshire, I really could not say.

THE TOWN'S GLORY
PONTYPOOL PARK

Pontypool can seem a rather drab workaday place, its town centre badly hit by the recession, but it boasts a vast and magnificent municipal park that Cardiff, Swansea or Newport can scarcely match.

Ponymoile Gates, Pontypool Park.

The park belonged to the wealthy industrialist Hanbury family and their fine house, which dates from 1659, still survives as the centrepiece of St Albans Roman Catholic High School, though it is much altered. The landscaped park has since 1920 been open for everyone to enjoy. There are ornamental trees, sweeping lawns, shady paths, a bizarre Victorian shell grotto and, for the more energetic, a modern sports and leisure centre. There is also the home ground of Pontypool Rugby Club – an impregnable stronghold in the glory days of the 'Pontypool Front Row' in the 1970s. In the Upper Park at Trevethin (*see* p.106) are the American Gardens, laid out in 1850, and the Folly Tower.

A path leads from the leisure centre to the magnificent eighteenth-century wrought-iron gates. These are said to have been a gift to John Hanbury by the Duchess of Marlborough for his services as Executor of the late Duke's will. They hang from ornate cast iron gate piers made in 1830 at the Blaenavon Works.

Recently these gates have been the subject of some controversy. They have been painted in a curious shade of faded green. The art historians that were consulted are convinced this is their original colour but most of the locals prefer the dignified black that they remember!

CHILDREN DREAM OF A GREENER FUTURE
COMMERCIAL STREET, PONTYPOOL

Young Pontypool teenagers were encouraged to look into the future for a Millennium Project art installation in Commercial Street that was unveiled by the Rt Hon. Paul Murphy, Secretary of State for Wales. The mural was created under the direction of artist Andrew Bolton, but their ideas were crucial.

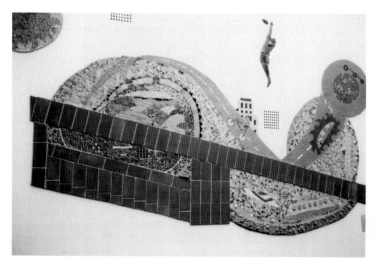

Millennium Mosaic, Commercial Street, Pontypool.

Pontypool's past was depicted as a child working underground in a mine and by the gates of a canal lock. The present is greener – artworks on a roundabout and cycle paths. The future is greener still, as the students' imaginations expanded – the canal, now beautifully clean, is in daily use as a means of transporting goods and people. Solar-powered cars glide silently past and Pontypool's Folly Tower has been converted into a theme park ride from which you can fly into the air!

Today's Pontypool does not quite live up to this vision yet – but you never know!

IRONMASTER DYNASTY COMMEMORATED

TREVETHIN

St Cadoc's Church, with its grand view southwards over Pontypool, is largely Victorian but it houses some older monuments to one of the area's most important iron-making families.

Originally from Worcestershire, the Hanburys first established ironworks in the Pontypool area in Elizabethan times but it was not until John Hanbury (born 1664) took control of the business that it really developed. He had married a rich heiress in 1701 and spent much of the wealth she brought to the marriage on modernising the works. He introduced various technical improvements and established Pontypool as a major centre of the industry. For the last fourteen years of his life he was Member of Parliament for Monmouthshire. It is said that in the House of Commons 'he spoke little but was much respected'.

John Hanbury died in 1734 and was buried at Trevethin. He is commemorated in St Cadoc's by an impressive black-veined marble memorial containing a bust by Rysbrack, a noted sculptor of the time. The church also contains memorials to many of his descendants and the family, now the Hanbury Tenisons, is still prominent today.

A sombre stained-glass window in the chancel is a memorial a colliery explosion at Llanerch in 1890. With its image of Christ receiving the sick and heavy laden, it commemorates the 181 local miners who died in the disaster.

Another memorial is to Thomas Davis James and W.R. Roberts. As Arthur Mee recalled 'they were cousins, sons of two sisters. They were born within a few weeks of each other, went to the same school and university, were ordained on the same Sunday by the same bishop – and died within two days of each other when they were only 27'.

Now on the edge of an extensive housing estate, Trevethin church is often locked. Its location is not what it was – but a path the Hanburys would still recognise leads through woods and fields back down to their former home in Pontypool Park. They travelled along this path in their carriage to attend services at Trevethin. Known as Herbert's Path, after a later owner of the woodland, it has recently been restored to its former condition.

Above left: Folly Tower (as seen on a mosaic at Crane Street in Pontypool).

Above right: St Cadoc's Church, Trevethin.

On the edge of Trevethin there is a folly tower, a replica (dating from 1993-4) of the one built by John Hanbury in 1762. This tower, which had been renovated in 1831, had been demolished at the beginning of the Second World War as it was feared that it would be a landmark for incoming German bombers! It stands near an early Victorian 'Rustic Lodge' in an extension of Pontypool Park, an area landscaped and planted as an American Garden in the 1850s.

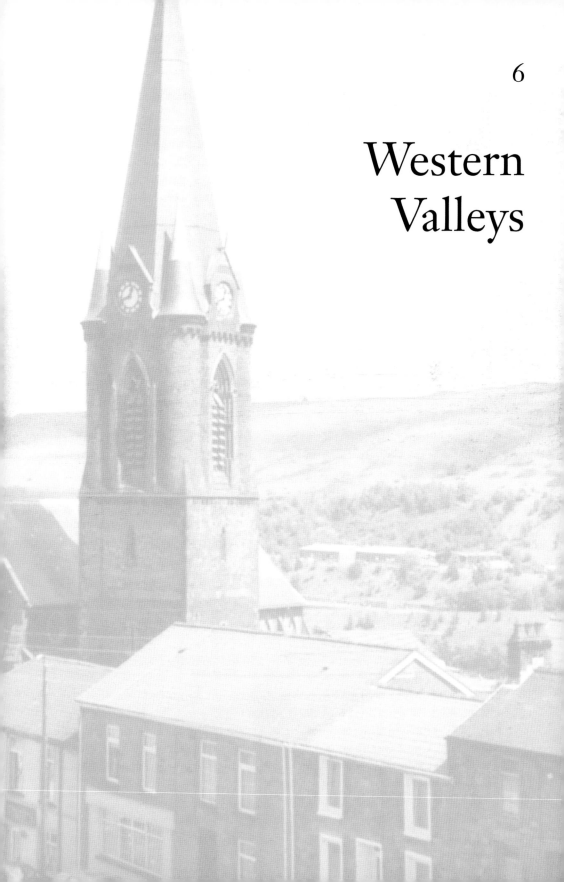

6

Western Valleys

TALE OF TWO CHURCHES

ABERCARN

The modern motorist sees little of Abercarn as he speeds past on the A467 between Risca and Newbridge. It seems to offer little of interest beyond its impressive wooded valley location, light industrial units and the depot of a large haulage company.

However, it does have a significant industrial history and a unique tale of two churches. Ironworking hereabouts goes back to the sixteenth century and the remains of a mid-eighteenth-century furnace survive to the east of the village on the side of the Nant Gwyddon. It is the earliest furnace to survive fairly intact on the South Wales coalfield. The first coalmines locally date from the early nineteenth century and the most important mine was the Prince of Wales Colliery, begun in 1862.

The major landowner around Abercarn was the eminent Parliamentarian, Sir Benjamin Hall, later Lord Llanover. A great champion of Welsh culture, he was particularly supportive of the use of the Welsh language in Christian worship. In support of this principle, in 1853 he paid for the building of a church on his estate at Abercarn. Set on a wooded hillside above the valley on the Afon Gwyddon, a tributary on the Ebbw, it is an impressive structure of Pennant sandstone.

Church life in Abercarn seems to have been quite complicated. In 1862, after a dispute with the Church of England (remember, Monmouthshire was an English county in those days), the church was handed over to the Calvinistic Methodists. The Anglicans eventually built a new church for themselves in the 1920s. In 1951 Arthur Mee described it as 'a magnificent modern church – standing like a fort, its tower like a castle keep and looking boldly across the valley to the mountains'. The tower is still a significant local landmark but in 1958 the building was found to be suffering structural defects due to the effects of subsidence. It was finally closed in the early 1980s. In a spirit of ecumenical co-operation which would have been unthinkable a century before, Anglicans and Methodists now share Lord Llanover's building.

Yet the shell of the 1920s church still survives. 'To enter its windowless hulk,' writes John Newman, 'is a powerful architectural experience. It stands high above the road from which a long flight of steps wanders up to the towering west front. It is an awesome sight.'

The churches are not easy to find as they are not signposted from the centre of the village. Eventually, I took the road that leads up from the High Street, past the Rechabite Hall with its moralistic text carved into the stonework. Opposite the school, whose children could be heard busily engaged in some activity, a path led up into the heavily-wooded churchyard of Lord Llanover's chapel. The sound of the children fell away and an eerie silence enveloped me. There was no notice board and nothing to indicate that this church was still in use.

Far left: The former Welsh church Abercarn, paid for by Sir Benjamin Hall.

Left: The ruins of St Luke's Anglican church, Abercarn.

Through the trees I caught a glimpse of the walls of the ruined Anglican church. To get there I had to go down the chapel's road access, turn right at the end and walk round the walled-off churchyard. The steps Newman wrote about are still there, their entrance boarded up (although there is a gap by which nefarious trespassers doubtless gain access). Further round there is a high metal security gate through which there is a good view of the gaunt, fortress-like structure.

It is a sinister spot, like a set for a horror film. It feels like all sorts of dark deeds could happen there and probably have. I took a photograph but then the battery on my camera mysteriously failed and I had to return to Newport to get a new one. I am not sure that I want to go back to Abercarn on my own!

MOSAIC COMMEMORATES INDUSTRIAL HERITAGE
ABERTILLERY

Abertillery's name comes from the Afon Tyleri, the small stream that here flows into the Little Ebbw Valley. The town owes its origin to the establishment of a tinplate works established here in 1846 and the coalmines that followed.

This industrial heritage is celebrated in a mosaic by Kenneth Budd that adorns the underpass beneath the new A467 road. The colourful panels include pictures of the tinplating process, coal mining and the railway – all of which have now gone, although the nearby Railway Inn recalls the days when the valley echoed to the sound of GWR locomotives working hard hauling heavy coal trains from the mines. It was all very different from the scene described by Archdeacon Coxe in 1799 and quoted in the Town Trail leaflet published by Blaenau Gwent Council:

Abertillery mosaic by
Kenneth Budd.

Thickly clothed with underwood and occasionally tufted with hanging
groves of oak, beech and alder; the wild raspberry twining in the thickets
and the ground overspread with the wood strawberry.

At Cwmtillery, a mile and a half to the north, there are two pit wheels set in a stone
base, put there in 1987 to mark the site of the colliery that was opened here in 1850.
Again the archdeacon painted a word-picture of the place before the great changes
wrought by industry took place, describing the valley as 'richly wooded and highly
cultivated, almost rivalling the fertile counties of England … numerous valleys
which abound with romantic scenery'. Crawshay Bailey, the ironmaster of Nantyglo
(*see* p.119), was attracted by the area's rural charms and rebuilt the farmhouse then
known as Llan-ty-Teri (now Gilfach Green) as a hunting lodge.

Now the slopes overlooking Cwmtillery are thickly wooded once again. Several
of the old farmhouses in the area survive largely unaltered and the two-mile circular
walk from the car park around the lakes and reservoir is well worth the effort!

TIMELINE OF INDUSTRIAL HISTORY
BLACKWOOD

Blackwood, now a bustling shopping centre between Newport and Tredegar, owed
its development to John Hodder Moggridge of Bradford-on-Avon in Wiltshire
who became a colliery owner locally around 1800. The first houses in the town
were built by him to accommodate his workers and he had an enviable reputation
as a man who treated his employees fairly. In 1805 the Sirhowy Valley Tramroad
was built to transport iron and coal from the ironworks at Tredegar down the
valley to Newport. Blackwood High Street follows the route of the tramway.

The town's history is recalled in the 'Blackwood Timeline', a series of nine bronze plaques designed by Michael Fairfax set into the pavement along the length of the High Street. It begins with the sparsely-populated pre-industrial settlement and ends with ideas of its future contributed by the children of Libanus Primary School.

These plaques are small, only 400mm square, and are easily missed in the busy street during the day. At night they are illuminated, giving off a warm glow. A leaflet, available at the library, includes descriptions of each one and a map showing where they are to be found.

Perhaps more noticeable are the examples of modern artwork that are a feature of the town centre. John Mills' 'Tower of Hands' proudly acknowledges the fact that '200 local residents had a hand in the making of this sculpture' (quite literally!). Nearby is his gentler and more colourful 'Singing Tree'. The palatial new bus station features the 'Dwarf Wall' and the Northern Gateway sculpture enigmatically marks the approach to the town along the A4048. The town is also known for its Miners Institute, built in 1925, now used as a theatre and cinema but looking rather drab and down-at-heel.

Blackwood was a centre of Chartism in the 1830s and it was from here, as well as Nantyglo and Pontypool, that the stalwart marchers set off, only to come to an unfortunate end outside the Westgate Hotel in Newport in November 1839.

The movement is commemorated by the name of the Chartists Bridge, that dramatic new viaduct that strides across the wooded Sirhowy Valley to the north of the town. The roundabout at the eastern end of the bridge is dominated by a giant glittering figure, pointing dramatically – another example of the modern artwork that enlivens Blackwood.

The 'Tower of Hands', Blackwood.

THE HIGHEST TOWN IN SOUTH WALES

BRYNMAWR

Brynmawr's name translates into English as 'Big Hill' and, at 1,200ft above sea level, the town claims to be the highest in South Wales. Today it is a bright and breezy place, spectacularly-located and retaining many monuments to its industrial past.

One of the most distinctive is also one of the newest but it is only a fragment of what existed until recently. In Warwick Road, leading west from the town centre, stood the Rubber Factory (later Dunlop Semtex). When it opened in 1947 it boasted the largest single-span concrete roof in the world. This spanned the enormous central production area using a network of thin-shell vaults. The building was celebrated in the 1951 Festival of Britain and hailed as the most inventive industrial building of the time.

The factory deserved preservation as an industrial monument but was demolished a few years ago to make way for a retail park that has not yet happened. All that was left by 2009 was the Boiler House, across the road to the east. This is in a derelict state but its paraboloid concrete roof is still an impressive landmark.

A small 1930s factory unit nearby housed a bootmaker's and was part of the 'Brynmawr Experiment', a self-help scheme devised by local Quakers to assist people during the Depression by creating employment. The Welfare Park, with its distinctive red-brick entrance, was built at the same time using Miners' Welfare Funds. It is on the site of ponds created to store water for the old Nantyglo Ironworks in the nineteenth century. The whole district was once criss-crossed by industrial tramways.

Above left: The rubber factory Boiler House (built 1947), Brynmawr.

Above right: Libanus Chapel, Brynmawr.

In the old part of Brynmawr a grid pattern of streets lined by terraced houses, pubs and chapels, recalls the town's past. Number 23 Chapel Street was once an inn, named after its landlord, a Chartist leader nicknamed 'King Crispin'. After the disaster of the Chartist March on Newport in 1839, he fled back to Brynmawr but was discovered hiding in a chest in the pub. Nearby is a small Chartist memorial stone.

In 1870, Chapel Street was the scene of a tragic accident. The owner of a warehouse sent a boy working for him into the cellar to fetch some stock. He took a candle to light his way, not knowing that the cellar contained barrels of gunpowder. A massive explosion resulted. Local legend states that half of his body was found that day and the rest of him three days later. A young girl playing close by was hit by falling debris and killed. The nearby Libanus and Calvary Chapels were badly damaged and had to be reinforced with iron stays. Rehoboth Chapel in King Street, erected in 1828, was the first nonconformist place of worship in Brynmawr. The Bardic Chair of Archdruid Crwys, once a Minister at Rehoboth, is on display inside the chapel whose keys can be obtained from the deacons on request.

A feature of Brynmawr's streets are the modern sculptures which enliven them. Some can be seen in the road that leads eastwards from the Market Hall (used as a cinema for over a century) and the Gwesty Bach Inn. This leads to the start of a spectacular long distance walk high above the Clydach Gorge, following the track of the old Heads of the Valleys railway towards Llanfoist and Abergavenny.

MEMORIAL TO SOUTH WALES MINERS
CWM

Standing proudly at the southern end of Cwm near Ebbw Vale, a 10ft-high statue of a miner commemorates the industry that shaped life in South Wales for more than a century.

It is not particularly easy for a stranger to find as it is not signposted from the centre of the village but it is worth the trek along the long straight street of well-maintained terraced houses. Head for the railway tunnel mouth visible in the distance and there you will find it, alongside the railway and the busy main road that now by-passes Cwm.

Beyond was the old Marine Colliery, one of the most productive on the coalfield. At its peak, just after the First World War, over 2,700 men were employed here. As late as the 1980s Marine and the nearby Six Bells collieries produced most of the coal needed for the massive steelworks at Llanwern. Geological problems ultimately led to closure in 1989. Marine's site, best seen from the trains on the recently-reopened Ebbw Vale line, has been cleared and lies empty still, the position of the former shafts marked by the winding gear wheels half-buried in the ground.

The statue was made by a local stonemason and the inscription reads 'In Memory of the men that worked and lost their lives in the Ebbw Fawr Mining Industry'. This is particularly poignant here because in 1927 fifty-two men were killed in a disaster at the Marine Colliery. There was a competition between local schools to write a poem about the effect of the mining industry in the Valleys. The winning poem by pupils from Waunlwyd and Cwm primary schools is mounted on the memorial's plinth.

The monument's unveiling in February 2009 was not without incident. The sheet covering the statue became entangled with its head and could not be shifted. Eleven-year-old Ben Morris from Waunlwyd came to the rescue, climbing up the statue to get it off.

There are plans for an even larger monument to the forty-five men who died in an explosion at Six Bells Colliery in 1960. A figure of a miner, rivalling in scale Anthony Gormley's 'Angel of the North', will be put up in Abertillery if all goes according to plan. It will be created by sculptor Sebastien Boyesen, whose work is such a feature of the centre of Newport and Blackwood, where he is responsible for the Chartist Memorial. It is hoped that the figure will be the centrepiece of the Ebbw Fach Trail from Llanhilleth to Brynmawr.

How much the physical scars of mining, if not the emotional ones, have healed can be seen at the Silvent Valley Nature Reserve, also at Cwm. Once a remote and wooded glade, by the late 1790s it was a busy industrial area with coal being dug out of shallow pits and drift mines and hauled along horse-tramways to the top of an incline above Cwm.

Miner's Memorial, Cwm.

For over 100 years the waste shale was dumped in the valley, forming mounds, some of which still survive. Gradually vegetation is recolonising these tips, undisturbed since 1916. The Silent Valley now boasts the highest beech wood in Britain and is a Site of Special Scientific Interest, managed by the Gwent Wildlife Trust and Blaenau Gwent Borough Council. It is clearly signposted from the A4046 and, with its combination of industrial archaeology and natural history interest, is well worth a visit.

Work is still going on. In 1981 the old industrial waste dump was licensed to accept domestic refuse. As this landfill site is filled, the area is being landscaped and will eventually become part of the nature reserve.

FORMER STEEL-MAKING TOWN
IN SEARCH OF A NEW ROLE
EBBW VALE

The name Ebbw Vale is synonymous with industrial South Wales. In 1969, as a geography undergraduate, I was taken on a guided tour of the massive steelworks that dominated the valley in those days. It was the most technically-advanced in Britain. Much of its work was diverted to Llanwern but tinplate production still continues. The remaining buildings can be viewed from Steelworks Road, which runs along the bottom of the valley below the main part of the town. The most impressive is the large red-brick building bearing a prominent four-sided clock-tower. This building housed the General Offices of the steelworks. Its foundation stone was laid in May 1914 and it was completed in 1920. Once the hub of one of the largest industrial installations in the world, it now stands next to a swathe of empty land that was being cleared for new uses when I visited in June 2009. At its north end, Steelworks Road passes under the Big Arch (also known as Newtown Bridge). This was originally built in 1813 for the horse tramroad that brought in the iron ore.

To the north of the town centre, going towards Beaufort and Rassau, is the recently-restored Gorsedd Circle, built to commemorate the National Eisteddfod held at Ebbw Vale in 1958. It was resited here in 1966. At the time of my visit the town was eagerly looking forward to the return of this prestigious cultural event in 2010.

The growth of Ebbw Vale dates from the establishment of the ironworks in 1790. Industrial building and housing development continued apace throughout the nineteenth century. It is said that by 1870 there were no less than twenty-one chapels in Ebbw Vale and Beaufort, which says a lot about the religious fervour of the people, but also reflects their proclivity for denominational disputation! Those surviving include Ebenezer Calvinistic Methodist (1850) in Station Road and Penuel Chapel (dated 1865) in Church Street, Briery Hill (which is now used as a Scout Hall).

Christ Church, Briery Hill, earned the title of 'The Cathedral of the Hills'. Its dramatic architecture illustrates the wealth the industry generated. The church dates from 1860 and the £60,000 needed to build it was paid by Abraham Darby IV of the Ebbw Vale Ironworks Company. The heads at the side of the main doors are said to be carved in his likeness. He was the great-grandson of the Abraham Darby who pioneered modern iron-making techniques at Coalbrookdale in Shropshire. It was intended to build the floors, roof and spire entirely of iron. This would have been a good advertisement for the company but this ambitious idea had to be abandoned. Its Victorian fittings are characteristic of their date.

Apart from the steelworks, the other major industry was coal mining, further down the valley at Victoria and Cwm, where rows of typical terraced houses remain. The mines all closed in the 1980s and are commemorated by the memorial at Cwm (*see* p.115). In 1991, as part of a programme of similar events intended to revitalise depressed industrial areas, the Welsh Garden Festival took place at Victoria. Most of the temporary buildings for this have now gone but the ornamental trees survive as well as a Japanese garden designed around two artificial lakes. Even more incongruous in this typically South Walian valley location is the late 1990s shopping centre, isolated a bus-ride away from anywhere and featuring two circular tent-like pavilions that look uncomfortably out-of-place! Otherwise it's all rather featureless but is, I suppose, an apt memorial to its time. Nearby the recently reopened railway from Cardiff to Ebbw Vale peters out a mile or so short of its objective. In 2009 the bus service linking the station with the town was withdrawn.

The most recent memorial to Ebbw Vale's past came in May the same year, when a new town centre clock was erected, the culmination of a town centre regeneration costing £2.5 million. Named 'Echoes' and designed by Marianne Forrest, it stands 11m high at the main road junction in Market Street. It is made of stainless steel, with its faces designed to resemble pithead wheels. The clock faces are perched on a support shaped like a horse's neck, deriving from the translation of Glyn Ebwy, 'Valley of the Wild Horses'.

Far left: Christ Church, Briery Hill, Ebbw Vale.

Left: 'Echoes' by Marianne Forrest, Ebbw Vale.

Scattered, apparently at random, below the clock are seven shiny chrome balls, up to 4ft high. Placed there as part of a £1 million enhancement scheme funded by the Welsh Assembly, they have proved controversial. During the (hardly tropical) summer of 2009, local people complained that you could 'fry an egg' on them and that people unwarily sitting on them were getting burned. Samantha Dighton, owner of a nearby café, complained to the *Argus* that 'they look terrible. They are just taking up space which could be used for the market. They are a complete waste of money and a health hazard!'

ROUND TOWERS RECALL INDUSTRIAL UNREST AT IRONWORKS
NANTYGLO

The end of the Napoleonic Wars led to a decline in demand for the products of the iron industry in South Wales, a major recession and great social unrest. The workers became increasingly fierce in defence of their livelihood and the ironmasters became seriously concerned for their own safety.

The ironworks at Nantyglo had been established in the 1790s as an offshoot of those at Blaenavon. The works was on the site now occupied by the modern buildings of Nantyglo Comprehensive School (itself threatened with closure in 2010). In 1811 it was leased by Joseph Bailey, nephew of Richard Crawshay of the Cyfarthfa Works at Merthyr Tydfil. It was the Baileys who had constructed two defensive roundhouses as the problems in the industry worsened. They built them in about 1816 as a place of refuge for loyal and trusted company workers, to protect them from their more militant comrades. That year serious rioting took place in Nantyglo, overwhelming the local militia. Reinforcements had to be summoned by the authorities to restore order. For almost a fortnight a unit of the Scots Greys were billeted in the stables alongside the two roundhouses.

The towers were certainly well-designed for their purpose. They had iron doors set into stone porches which were covered by spiked canopies to prevent any rioters gaining access to the upper floors. The doors had holes through which muskets could be poked by the defenders if necessary. These holes could be sealed from the inside by hinged flaps. The towers also contained well-ventilated cellars where provisions could be stored in preparation for a lengthy siege. Window casements and other fittings normally made of wood were here constructed using cast iron – a material in cheap and plentiful supply in Nantyglo at the time. The roofs were made of cast-iron plates fixed around a circular central plate.

Nothing was left to chance, but the defensive capabilities of the round towers were never seriously challenged, despite further disorder in 1822 and the Chartist Risings of the late 1830s. By 1841 the southern tower was the residence of the Baileys' private secretary.

The Roundhouse, Nantyglo.

This tower is now in ruins but the northern one has recently been restored. The towers are not easy to find, despite being signposted off the main road through the village. As is so often the case, the brown tourist signs point confidently but then abandon the unfortunate visitor in a maze of lanes with no further information. There is a small parking area, part of a rough track that branches off Waun Ebbw Road on the western edge of the village, opposite a modern bungalow called 'Hawthorn'.

Even then it is not easy to approach the towers. Roundhouse Farm, with its interesting group of late eighteenth-century outbuildings, is privately-owned and not open to visitors. The towers, which are at either end of the complex, can only be viewed from the bridle path to the west of the site. It suddenly seems a very remote and mysterious spot. From this path a track leads to the ruins of Ty Mawr, the ornate mansion built by the Baileys in about 1820. This house was in use until 1885 and demolished during the Second World War.

A NEW BRIDGE, APTLY-NAMED

NEWBRIDGE

Outside its immediate district, the Valleys town of Newbridge is probably best known for two things: The 'Newbridge Memo' – one of those vast Workingmen's Institutes that are a feature of South Wales towns – and Champion boxer, Joe Calzaghe.

In April 2009, it was decided that the new footbridge nearing completion next to Newbridge School should be named after Mr Calzaghe, who was unbeaten in forty-six professional bouts when he retired the previous year.

In an intriguing mixture of Welsh, Italian and English, the structure has been named 'Pont Calzaghe Bridge' to honour the achievements of Joe and his father (and trainer) Enzo. The decision to do so was made by Caerphilly Borough Council whose deputy leader, Allan Pritchard, told the *Argus* that 'this famous boxing family has helped put Newbridge firmly on the map. They are ambassadors for the County Borough on a world stage.' The bridge crosses the railway line and

The new footbridge under construction and the railway station at Newbridge.

the River Ebbw and makes the town centre more accessible to pedestrians. Its futuristic design quickly raised it to the status of iconic local landmark. Father and son officially opened the bridge on 9 September.

Not that Newbridge is short of landmarks. The Newbridge Memo, dating from 1924, found national fame in the BBC television *Restoration* series in 2004 and its band of supporters are still working hard to ensure that this magnificent edifice survives and finds new community uses.

PIONEER 'MODEL VILLAGE' FOR MINEWORKERS
OAKDALE

The magnificent new Chartists' Bridge from Blackwood leads towards Oakdale, a pioneer 'Model Village' dating from the early years of the twentieth century, situated on the ridge of high ground to the east of the river and described by John Newman as 'by far the most ambitious attempt by any mining company in South Wales to provide planned housing for its workforce.'

The Tredegar Iron and Coal Company held a competition in 1910-11 to choose a designer for its estate of 660 houses for workers at the nearby colliery. Doubtless to the chagrin of the eventual winner, the result of the competition was ignored and the architect appointed was Mr A.F. Webb, who just happened to be the brother-in-law of the company's managing director.

Mr Webb's radical design for the estate shows up very clearly on maps and aerial photographs. Instead of the linear ribbon-development of the typical South Wales mining settlements, we have a broad central axis road, intersected by transverse streets, some of them describing mirror-image curves on either side. The shops are in the centre of the community, facing a well-wooded linear open space. The layout of the estate and the design of the houses, which are mostly arranged in short terraces, shows the influence of the 'Garden City' movement exemplified in England by Letchworth and Welwyn.

The Presbyterian church, Oakdale.

The churches, such as the Presbyterian church of 1916 in Penmean Avenue, stand at prime sites at the intersections of the major avenues and are key to the design, although the Anglican church of 1955 is clearly an afterthought. They are well-maintained, but the other public buildings have not been so fortunate. The Workman's Institute has been demolished but can be seen re-erected as the Welsh Folk Museum at St Fagans near Cardiff. The pub – gabled, tile-hung and pargetted in Arts & Crafts style – was closed and boarded-up when I visited the village.

In May 2009 a sculpture was unveiled to mark Oakdale's centenary. The memorial, called 'Coal Face' and 2.4m high, was created by Scottish artist Malcolm Robertson to reflect the area's mining tradition. Cast in bronze, it is in the shape of a miner's face, with the faces of fifteen local miners engraved into it. They include Caerphilly's mayor, John Evans, and Allan Pritchard, deputy leader of the Council. From the front their faces are seen in detail but from the back the sculpture resembles the raw coal-face.

In the planning and design of the memorial Mr Robinson consulted retired miners, residents and local schoolchildren. The monument is located in the square in the centre of the village.

MYSTERY OF BRAVERY MEDAL ON THE *ANTIQUES ROADSHOW*
PENGAM

Pengam is a former mining community right on the county boundary, once the border between England and Wales. It once had two stations on different lines on opposite sides of the Rhymney River. To distinguish them from each other they were known as Pengam (Mon) and Pengam (Glam).

Most local men worked at the Britannia Colliery in nearby Blackwood. One such was Lewis Phillips whose courageous actions and quick thinking underground on 15 June 1933 led to his being awarded a medal, known as the

Order of Industrial Heroism, popularly known as 'the Workers' VC'. This award was sponsored by the *Daily Herald*, the newspaper of the Trades Union Congress. (It was first awarded following an incident in which four workers helped to control a fire at the docks in Liverpool.)

Lewis Phillips was working with Richard Sheppard on a coal-cutting machine, a device involving a high-speed revolving drum bearing a series of sharp picks. Somehow, in the confined space underground, Mr Sheppard's arm and body were caught in the drum which continued to spin. Reaching over just in time, and at great risk to his own safety, Mr Phillips managed to stop the machine, saving his friend's life.

For the rest of his life he kept the medal in a biscuit barrel at home, but he never spoke about what he had done to earn it. Not knowing the story, his daughter, Gill Weatherhead, took the medal and accompanying certificate to a recording of the *Antiques Roadshow* in Somerset and with the help of the programme's experts and information from viewers, the story was pieced together.

The medal was presented at a ceremony at the Miners' Hall in Pengam, but even for this prestigious occasion the Institute's strict 'men only' rule was not relaxed. No women, not even members of Mr Phillips' family, were allowed in. Gill remembers that her father came home from the presentation a little the worse for wear. 'It was the only time I ever saw my father drunk,' she told the *Western Daily Press*. Sadly, the family do not even have any pictures of the event – Lewis was too shy to have any photographs taken. He died fifteen years later from kidney failure, aged just forty-eight.

The imposing sandstone 'Pengam & Fleur-de-Lis Workmen's Library and Institute', built in 1911, still stands in the High Street of Fleur-de-Lis, a settlement whose unusual name is supposed to come from a local inn – although some romantics claim it derives from an influx of Huguenot weavers!

Pengam and Fleur-de-Lis Workmen's Library and Institute (built 1911).

PAST INDUSTRIAL GLORIES

RISCA

With the exception of the names of some of its pubs, remains of its heavy industrial heritage are hard to find now, but Risca, a few miles inland from Newport, has an honourable place in the history of ironworking in South Wales. By 1900 the Monmouthshire Steel & Tinplate Works at Pontymister was a major employer and contributed to the rapid increase in population in the district.

The dramatic developments had begun a century before. In 1747 John Wesley wrote of passing through 'a little village at the foot of the hills, called Risca' but by 1801 Archdeacon Coxe wrote 'on my way to Risca I passed over a rail road, lately formed by Mr Edward Jones who rents some mines of lead, calamine and coal in Machen Hill on the opposite sides of the Ebwy'. The construction of the Monmouthshire Canal from Newport to Crumlin in 1796 and the Sirhowy Tramroad in 1805 accelerated the industrialisation of the valley. The construction of the tramroad necessitated the building of a thirty-two-arch viaduct at Risca, the so-called 'Long Bridge', but this was demolished in the early twentieth century and only a small part of the eastern abutment survives, a quarter of a mile south of the parish church.

Mines established around 1800 in the area were by mid-century supplying coal under contract to the ships of the Royal West India Steam Packet Company and the Peninsula & Orient and East India companies. Most collieries in South Wales were in the valleys, but at Risca a mine was sunk at the top of a ridge to exploit the Black Vein seam, reputedly the richest in the country.

In 1846 thirty-five men were killed in an explosion at the Black Vein Colliery. At the inquest it was alleged that the management had tried to get the men to use safety lamps but that they obstinately preferred to use candles! Another 146 men were killed in an explosion in 1860. It took two months to recover all the bodies. A century later, in an article on Risca in *Presenting Monmouthshire*, Geoffrey J. Williams wrote that 'the small graveyard in which the victims were interred can be seen forlorn and neglected above the canal near the former Green Meadow Inn'.

Above left: Pub name recalling industrial heritage, the Rolling Mill, Risca.

Above right: Chemist's shop interior from Cardiff and railway memorabilia, Oxford House Industrial museum.

In 1977 the Oxford House Industrial History Society was set up to study the town's heritage. It was officially inaugurated by Wynford Vaughan Thomas. In the mid-1990s the society was able to establish an industrial museum in the former Risca Collieries Workmen's Institute. This houses exhibits relating to the Sirhowy Tramroad and the Long Bridge and the later railways in the area, as well as a historic chemist's shop and memorabilia of working-class life. The museum is open on Saturdays in summer, from 10 a.m. to 12.30 p.m., and at other times by arrangement. The society also holds a series of lectures and meetings on Friday evenings. Details can be obtained on www.riscamuseum.org. uk. The Institute building itself dates from 1915 and is at the junction of St Mary Street and Grove Road.

THE ANEURIN BEVAN TRAIL
TREDEGAR

Aneurin Bevan's memory is still honoured in Tredegar, which was his birthplace on 15 November 1897, the fourth son in a family of ten children. Nye, as he became universally known, was to become one of the pre-eminent figures of twentieth-century socialism – the father of the National Health Service.

The Aneurin Bevan Heritage Trail, devised by Blaenau Gwent County Borough Council, takes in most of the landmarks of his early life in Tredegar, ending on the mountainside where his ashes, and those of his wife Jennie Lee, were scattered. The site overlooks a beautiful wooded valley at the head of the Duffryn Crawnon.

Number 32 Charles Street, the house where Nye was born, was demolished long ago and the Maes-y-Derwen residential home now stands on its site. The workmen's hall and library, where he was such an avid reader as a boy, are gone too (now a car park next to the Masonic Hall, and the official start of the trail), but Bedwellty House still stands in its park close to the town centre.

Bedwellty House was the home of the Tredegar Urban District Council, to which Nye Bevan was elected in 1922. His biographer, the former Labour leader Michael Foot, writes of the impact of the young socialist firebrand: 'He did not take his seat but erupted', challenging comfortable conventions with a passionate concern for the working people he represented.

'People are living in conditions not fit for criminals,' the *Argus* quoted at the time. 'No doubt horses, especially racehorses, are housed better than some of our citizens'. A portrait of Aneurin Bevan now hangs in the Assembly Rooms; there is also a bronze bust by Lambda. These can be seen by arrangement with the Town Clerk. Michael Foot, Nye's successor as MP for Ebbw Vale (and later for Blaenau Gwent) is also honoured in Tredegar and the house where he lived can be seen just up the hill from Bedwellty House.

Tredegar Social Club. The clock tower is made of cast iron and was erected in 1858.

A rare curiosity at Bedwellty House is a 15-ton block of coal which was intended for display at the Great Exhibition in 1851. Raising it safely to the surface must have been an epic feat, but the logistics of actually getting it to London obviously defeated Tredegar's best minds! A project to restore the gardens, due to take several years, was in progress when I visited Tredegar and they were not accessible.

Aged thirty-one, Bevan was elected Labour MP for Ebbw Vale in 1929. The balcony of the Tredegar Social Club (overlooking the clock tower) was where the result of the count would be announced to cheering crowds on Election Night. At Westminster he met and subsequently married Jennie Lee, who was his equal in her fervour for the cause of socialism. Nye was editor of *Tribune*, the Left's newspaper, from 1942 to 1945. He was elected to the Labour Party National Executive in 1944 and became Minister of Health in the Atlee government in 1945. He was largely responsible for the establishment of the National Health Service and also launched Britain's largest-ever programme of council houses. His latter years were overshadowed by illness and he died in July 1960, mourned by political friends and foes alike.

Out of town, on the high ground between Tredegar and Ebbw Vale, are the Aneurin Bevan Memorial Stones. These were erected to mark the place where he held open-air meetings. He was famed as a powerful and eloquent public speaker. The centre stone represents Nye himself and the others point to the three towns of his constituency: Ebbw Vale, Tredegar and Rhymney.

Across the busy A4047 from the car park is the start of the twenty-six-mile Sirhowy Valley Walk. This is appropriate as Nye and Bevan loved walking in this area. This path leads along disused railway lines, woodland tracks and country lanes to pass under the Chartist Bridge at Blackwood. On the way it passes Hollybush where James James, the composer of 'Land of My Fathers', was born at the Ancient Druid Inn in 1832. From Blackwood it climbs towards Mynydd Machen and then down to Rhiwderin, ending at Tredegar House, Newport.

Far Off Things

Along with Newport-born poet W.H. Davies, Caerleon's Arthur Machen (born 1863) best captures the charms of Monmouthshire. In his autobiography, *Far Off Things*, Machen (quoted by Arthur Mee) recalls his early memories:

> To the eastward the bedroom window of Llandewi Rectory looked out over hills and valleys, away to the forest of Wentwood and the church tower on the hill above Caerleon. Through a cleft one might see now and again a bright yellow glint of Severn Sea and the cliffs of Somerset beyond. And hardly a house in sight in all the landscape.
>
> Here the gable of a barn, here a glint of a whitewashed farmhouse, here blue woodsmoke rising from an orchard grove, where an old cottage was snugly hidden. And of nights, when the dusk fell and the farmer went on his rounds, you might chance to see his lantern glimmering a very spark on the hillside.

His contemporary, W.H. Davies (born 1871), is best remembered for his memoir of life on the road in America, *Autobiography of a Super-Tramp*, but for me his best work is the lyrical poetry written later in life. He seems to have been happiest writing about the sights and sounds of the Monmouthshire countryside:

> What is this life, if full of care
> We have no time to stand and stare?

I sometimes think that these two lines sum up my philosophy of life. I do a lot of standing and staring these days. In the contrasting parts of Monmouthshire there are certainly many curiosities worth staring at!

The author admires the view of the Usk Valley (from the road from St Arvans to Trellech).

Other local titles published by The History Press

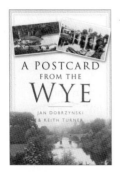

A Postcard from the Wye
JAN DOBRZYNSKI & KEITH TURNER

A Postcard from the Wye takes the reader on a journey in words and pictures along the entire length of the river, using more than 200 postcards from the authors' extensive collections. It is a record of how the river once was, including its industrial heritage as well as more rural scenes, and shows how it was immortalised by earlier generations of photographers and artists for the benefit of innumerable tourists and travellers.

978 0 7509 4850 0

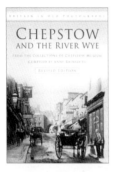

Chepstow and the River Wye In Old Photographs
CHEPSTOW MUSEUM

Through the photographs in this album the viewer may travel around the town of Chepstow, cross the river to Beachley, Sedbury and Tutshill, and voyage up the Wye to Tintern stopping, like tourists of old, to look at Piercefield and explore the Wyndcliff. This selection of photographs, drawn from collections at Chepstow Museum, focuses as much on the people – working, playing and celebrating – as it does on the place.

978 0 7524 5019 3

Abergavenny Pubs
FRANK OLDING

Using images held in the archives of the Abergavenny Museum, this illustrated volume of the town's pubs traces the development of the licensed trade in this area of Wales. Abergavenny Pubs will delight all those who want to know more about the history of the town's pubs, their clientele, landlords and ladies.

978 0 7524 3576 3

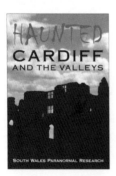

Haunted Cardiff and the Valleys
SOUTH WALES PARANORMAL RESEARCH

Journey through the darker side of Cardiff and the surrounding valleys, an area steeped in ancient history and ghostly goings-on. Drawing on extensive research and interviews with first-hand witnesses, South Wales Paranormal Research have put together this chilling collection of sightings and mysterious happenings, mostly from the last ten years. Featuring ghostly cars and ships, mysterious policemen and figures in country lanes, this book will appeal to everyone interested in the paranormal.

978 0 7524 4378 2

Visit our website and discover thousands of other History Press books.
www.thehistorypress.co.uk